Bridge Play for Beginners

by the same author

*

FIRST BOOK OF BRIDGE

Bridge Play
for Beginners

by

ALFRED SHEINWOLD

FABER AND FABER
3 Queen Square
London

First published in England in 1955
by Faber and Faber Limited
3 Queen Square London W.C.1.
First published in this edition 1970
Reprinted 1972 and 1978
printed in Great Britain by
Whitstable Litho Ltd Whitstable Kent
All rights reserved

ISBN 0 571 09528 3

Contents

CONTENTS

CONTENTS

Glossary

AVOIDANCE: a play that is intended to prevent the dangerous opponent from gaining the lead.

BATH COUP: the play of a low card by declarer when he holds A-J-x and when the opening lead is the king of a suit.

BLOCK: to win a trick in the wrong hand with the result that you cannot continue to play a long suit.

CASH: to take a sure trick at once rather than later on.

CLEAR A SUIT: to establish a suit by forcing the opponents to play their high cards.

COMMUNICATION: the means of leading from one partnership hand to the other.

COVER: to play a higher card than one previously played in the trick. The expression is used especially of honours, as in 'covering an honour with an honour'.

CROSS-RUFF: a series of tricks in which declarer trumps one suit in his own hand and another suit in the dummy.

DECLARER: the player of the team with the winning bid who was first to name the suit (or no-trump) and who plays the hand.

DEFENDER: either of the two partners who play against declarer.

DISCARD: to play a card of a suit (not the trump suit) that is different from the suit led.

DOUBLETON: an original holding of only two cards in a suit.

DRAW TRUMPS: to lead the trump suit until the defenders have no more trumps left.

DROP: to capture an opponent's high card by playing a higher card of your own, on which his must fall.

DUCK: to play low instead of winning a trick, especially when your purpose is to save your entry until it is most useful to you.

DUMMY: declarer's partner; also, the hand of declarer's partner.

DUMMY REVERSAL: the establishment of the dummy instead of your own hand, especially by ruffing dummy's losers with your own trumps.

ECHO: a method of signalling. (See High-Low.)

ENDPLAY: a play that makes an opponent lead to your benefit.

ENTRY: a card that can win a trick and thus provide the right to lead on the next trick.

EQUALS: two or more cards in unbroken order of rank, e.g. K-Q-J or Q-J, etc. Same as sequence, or touching cards.

ESTABLISH: to promote low cards to winning rank.

FALSE CARD: to play a higher card than necessary in order to deceive an opponent.

FINESSE: an attempt to win a trick with a card that is not the highest playable card of its suit.

FOLLOW SUIT: to play a card of the suit that has been led.

FORCE: to lead a card that compels an opponent (especially the declarer) to ruff.

FORCE OUT: to make an opponent take a winning card by leading a lower card in the suit.

HIGH-LOW: a method of signalling (by playing first high and then low) used by the defenders to show strength or to ask that a suit be led again. Same as echo.

HOLD-UP: to play a low card instead of winning the trick, especially for the purpose of destroying an opponent's entry.

LEAD: to play the first card of any trick; also, the first card of a trick.

LEAD AWAY FROM: to lead a low card from a suit headed by one or more high cards, as 'to lead away from a king'.

LEAD THROUGH: to lead a suit that is likewise held by the opponent who plays next, as 'to lead through strength'.

LEAD TOWARDS: to lead a suit that is likewise held by your partner, as 'to lead towards a king'.

LONG CARDS: the cards that are left when neither opponent still has any card in the suit; the surviving cards.

LONG SUIT: a suit with four or more cards; a suit that may produce 'long cards'.

LOSERS: cards that are likely to lose tricks.

MAJOR SUIT: spades or hearts.

MINOR SUIT: diamonds or clubs.

OPEN: to make the first lead of a hand; sometimes also used of a later lead that is the first lead in its suit.

OPEN UP: to play a suit in such a way as to risk losing tricks in it; to use up your stoppers in a suit.

OPENING LEAD: the first lead of a hand.

OVER-TAKE: to win a trick that would otherwise be won by your partner's high card.

OVER-TRICK: a trick in excess of the contract.

GLOSSARY

PLAIN SUIT: see Side Suit.

RETURN: to lead after winning the previous trick; also, to lead the same suit previously led by your partner.

RUFF: to play a trump on a side suit when you cannot follow suit. Same as to trump.

RUFFER: a card that can be used for ruffing; a ruffing trick.

SEQUENCE: two or more cards in unbroken order of rank, e.g. K-Q-J, or Q-J, etc. Same as equals.

SET: to defeat a contract.

SET UP: to promote low cards to winning rank. Same as to establish.

SHIFT: to lead a different suit.

SHORT HAND: the partnership hand that has fewer cards in a particular suit.

SHORT SUIT: a suit in which fewer than three cards are held.

SHOW OUT: to fail to follow suit; to discard.

SIDE SUIT: any suit other than the trump suit. Same as plain suit.

SIGNAL: a play made to inform your partner.

SINGLETON: an original holding of only one card in a suit.

SLUFF: to discard.

SLUFF AND RUFF: to ruff in one of the partnership hands while discarding a loser from the other hand.

SQUEEZE: to force the opponents to make damaging discards, especially by running a long suit.

STOPPER: a card that will sooner or later take a trick in a suit.

TENACE: a combination in one hand of the best and third-best cards (such as A-Q) still in play.

TOP-OF-NOTHING: a lead of the highest of three worthless cards in a suit.

TOUCHING CARDS: two or more cards in unbroken order of rank. Same as sequence, or equals.

TRUMP: to play a trump card on a suit in which you are void.

TRUMP CONTRACT: a contract in a suit, not no-trump.

UNBLOCK: to play a higher card than necessary in order to save a low card of the suit for later use.

VOID SUIT: an original holding of no cards in a suit.

WIDE OPEN: without a stopper.

WINNERS: cards that are expected to win tricks.

x: any unimportant low card in a suit. For example, K-x means the king and a low card of the suit.

ONE

Before You Begin

This book is about the play of the cards at contract bridge. It assumes that you know something about bidding, and that you have played a little bridge—enough to get the 'feel' of the cards. Now you want to learn to play the cards *well*.

What can you learn from a book about playing the cards? After all, there are millions and millions of possible hands—and even a very big book could show only a few hundred hands. Besides, would you have the patience to read such a big book?

Don't worry; you can learn. Thousands of bridge players have already learned something about the play of the cards from newspaper articles and books. If they can do it, you can do it too.

The most helpful fact is that bridge hands tend to resemble one another. If you learn the best way to play a certain hand you will automatically know how to play all hands that closely resemble it. Hence, a few principles of play will equip you to get good results out of most bridge hands.

Bridge is more enjoyable, however, if you are willing to do just a little thinking, too. You don't have to be a genius; most good bridge players are perfectly average people with only average brain-power. You merely have to think in straight lines instead of all round the mulberry bush. You'll be amazed at how simple it really is.

For example, everybody knows that there are thirteen cards in each suit. Suppose that the first three tricks of a hand are all spades, with all four players following suit on all three tricks. Wouldn't you then know that only one of the original thirteen spades is left *un*played?

Surprisingly enough, most bridge players don't bother with simple arithmetic, or maybe they can't remember from one trick to another what has been played. That's why most bridge players play their cards very badly.

It's going to be different in *your* case. This book can't do your thinking for you, but it will teach you how to think and what to think about. If you learn that, you will have a tremendous advantage over nine-tenths of all the bridge players in the world!

How to Use This Book

In all of the hands in this book, South is the declarer and North is the dummy. The bidding is given in each case, but there is neither comment on nor explanation of the bidding. You will find that the contract is always logical and that it is arrived at by logical steps.

If you want to refresh your memory on the values shown by various bids, the table on the next page will help you.*

One final word of advice. Don't try to read this book all in one sitting. A few hands at a time are all that you can easily digest. And when you have reached the end of the

---

* If you want more information on bidding, you may want to turn back to my *First Book of Bridge*, in which bidding and point count are thoroughly explained.

book by slow stages you will find that some of the earlier hands, which may have seemed difficult on first reading, will then seem easy and self-evident.

When you get to that stage you will be a very good bridge player!

POINT COUNT BIDDING

OPENING BIDS

Points

12 or 13, good suit	1 of suit
14, any suit	1 of suit
16 to 18, stoppers	1 NT
22 to 24, stoppers	2 NT
25 to 27, stoppers	3 NT
25 or more, good suit	2 of suit

RESPONSES TO 1 OF SUIT

6 to 16	1 of new suit
9 to 16	2 of lower suit
17 or more	Jump, new suit
6 to 10, trumps	Raise to 2
13 to 16, trumps	Raise to 3
8 or less, trumps, void or singleton	Raise to 4
6 to 9	1 NT
13 to 15, stoppers	2 NT
16 or 17, stoppers	3 NT

RESPONSES TO 1 NT

0 to 7	Pass or 2 of long suit
8 or 9	2 NT
10 to 15	3 NT or 3 of long suit
16 or more	Aim for slam

POINT COUNT	
Ace	4
King	3
Queen	2
Jack	1

KEY NUMBERS	
Game	26 points
Small Slam	33 points
Grand Slam	37 points

TWO

Play at No-trumps

Sometimes you can win all the tricks that you need by the simple process of taking one high card after another. If so, don't make a big fuss about the hand: take your tricks and get on to the next hand.

1.

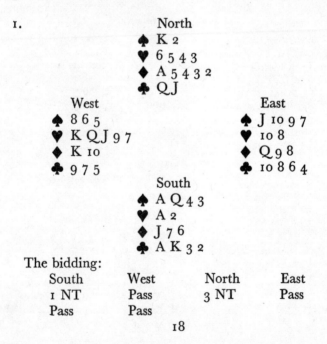

North
♠ K 2
♥ 6 5 4 3
♦ A 5 4 3 2
♣ Q J

West
♠ 8 6 5
♥ K Q J 9 7
♦ K 10
♣ 9 7 5

East
♠ J 10 9 7
♥ 10 8
♦ Q 9 8
♣ 10 8 6 4

South
♠ A Q 4 3
♥ A 2
♦ J 7 6
♣ A K 3 2

The bidding:

South	West	North	East
1 NT	Pass	3 NT	Pass
Pass	Pass		

West leads the king of hearts, and your partner puts the North hand down on the table as the dummy. You are South, and it is up to you to make your contract of 9 tricks for three no-trumps.

What should you do first? It's easier to tell you what *not* to do. Don't do *anything* until you've given the whole hand a moment's thought.

It's perfectly true that you'll eventually have to play one of dummy's low hearts, and that it won't make any difference which of those low cards you play from the dummy at the first trick. Just the same, it is important for you to get into the habit of making a plan before you play the first card from the dummy—no matter how obvious that first play may be.

How do you make a plan? Your first step is to count your tricks.

If you choose to do so, you can win the first trick with the ace of hearts in your own hand. You will then be in position to win three additional tricks with the ace, king, and queen of spades; one trick with the ace of diamonds; and four tricks with the ace, king, queen, and knave of clubs. Nine tricks in all.

Don't be in a hurry to take my word for it. Look at the diagram of the hand and see for yourself that each of those cards can win a trick. Better still, take a pack of cards and lay out the hand. Some players find it easier to work with the actual playing cards than with a diagram in a book.

Since nine tricks will give you your contract of three no-trumps you decide to take your nine tricks and save your brains for another hand.

WIN IN THE SHORT HAND FIRST

You don't need great skill to take nine tricks in high

cards. Still, it is quite possible to tie yourself up into a knot even on so simple a hand. Let's take the tricks the right way, and then see what pitfalls you have avoided.

You win the first trick with the ace of hearts. You lead the deuce of clubs, and dummy wins with the knave. You lead the queen of clubs from dummy and play the three of clubs from your own hand.

Next you lead the king of spades from dummy and follow suit with the three of spades from your hand. You continue with the deuce of spades from the dummy, winning with the queen of spades in your own hand. Now you are able to lead, in succession, the ace of spades, the ace of clubs, and the king of clubs. Finally, you lead a low diamond to dummy's ace, and cheerfully give up the rest of the tricks to the enemy. You have taken your nine tricks.

It was so easy that perhaps you didn't notice how you could have made a mistake. Let's suppose that you do it the *wrong* way.

You take the first trick with the ace of hearts, lead a low club to dummy's knave, and cash dummy's queen. So far, so good. Now you do something very foolish. You lead dummy's low spade to your own ace, and a low spade back to dummy's king.

Do you see what has happened? You are stuck (blocked) in the dummy, with no way to get to your own hand for the queen of spades and the ace and king of clubs. Now you cannot take your nine tricks, and you will be defeated.

This hand teaches you the first rule of playing the cards: Take the early tricks in the *short* hand and the later tricks in the *long* hand. In this case, dummy is *short* in spades (only two cards) while the South hand is *long* (four cards). Hence the first spade trick must be taken in the dummy (the *short* hand).

Now that you have seen the first hand of the book you

can begin to prepare yourself for the rest of the hands. Each hand will teach you at least one important lesson and will show you the direction your thoughts ought to take when you come up against a similar hand in a regular game of bridge.

In order to make the most out of these hands, you will probably have to play them through more than once. Don't let that discourage you. Of the hundreds of bridge players that I have taught, not one absorbed every single point the first time it was mentioned. Everybody needs a certain amount of repetition.

You may find that the diagrams in this book don't give you the 'feel' of a real game. If so, lay out each hand with a pack of cards, and then follow the play with the actual cards instead of with the printed page.

If you use playing cards, don't play the cards of each trick in the middle of the table. As a card is played from each hand, turn it over face down, and let it stay with the hand from which it came. At the end of the play, you'll have thirteen cards turned face down for each hand, and you can easily turn them face up again in order to repeat the play. Likewise, if you want to stop in the middle of the play, you'll find it very easy to turn up the cards that are face down and begin all over again.

If you find it convenient to use the book instead of laying out the actual playing cards, it is easy to solve the problem of replaying a hand. Keep a pencil in your hand, and draw a light slanting line through each card as it is played. Slant all the lines in the same direction. When you want to try the hand again, draw a line that slants in the opposite direction. By the time you have played a hand twice, each hand will be crossed out lightly with a pencilled 'X'.

You can then play the hand a third time by drawing a ring round each card as it is played. Then an eraser will get rid of all the marks, and you'll be able to approach the hand with a fresh mind.

Whichever way you play the hands, be sure to play them all out from start to finish. The practice will be good for you.

ESTABLISHING A LONG SUIT

2.

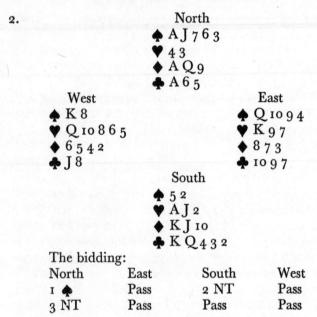

North
♠ A J 7 6 3
♥ 4 3
♦ A Q 9
♣ A 6 5

West
♠ K 8
♥ Q 10 8 6 5
♦ 6 5 4 2
♣ J 8

East
♠ Q 10 9 4
♥ K 9 7
♦ 8 7 3
♣ 10 9 7

South
♠ 5 2
♥ A J 2
♦ K J 10
♣ K Q 4 3 2

The bidding:

North	East	South	West
1 ♠	Pass	2 NT	Pass
3 NT	Pass	Pass	Pass

West leads the six of hearts, and your first step—as we have seen before—is to sit still and think before you play the first card from the dummy.

You begin by counting your tricks. You can surely win tricks with the ace of spades, the ace of hearts, the three top diamonds, and the three top clubs. The total is eight tricks.

22

Notice that you can win only three diamond tricks even though you have the six highest diamonds between your own hand and the dummy. Unfortunately for you, when dummy takes the ace of diamonds you will have to play one of your own good diamonds on it; and when you play the king one of dummy's good diamonds will have to be played on it; and so on.

You have only eight tricks in high cards, and you need nine tricks to make three no trumps. Hence you must *develop* a trick.

Your plan is to *establish* one or more of the low clubs so that you can win a trick with it. You can do this by making the opponents play all of their clubs; and then any low club that you happen to have left will win a trick when you lead it.

Having made the plan, you put it into operation. You win the first trick with the ace of hearts and lead the deuce of clubs to dummy's ace. (Note that the first club trick is taken in the *short* hand.) West has to play the eight of clubs, and East must follow suit with the seven of clubs.

You return a low club from dummy to your king, dropping West's knave and East's nine of clubs. Now you lead the queen of clubs, and East must follow suit with his ten. This exhausts all of the clubs held by the opponents. Your four and three of clubs are the last two cards of that suit.

Making the most of your good luck, you lead the four of clubs, winning a trick with it; and then you lead the three of clubs. On these two tricks you discard two low spades from the dummy, and you don't really care what the opponents discard. You are ready to take the ace of spades and three diamond tricks, making your contract plus an over trick.

FORCING OUT AN ACE

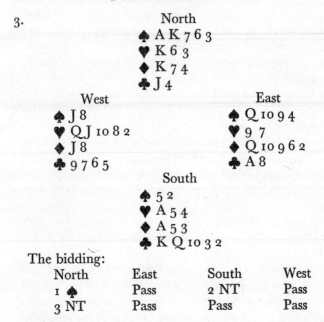

3.

North
♠ A K 7 6 3
♥ K 6 3
♦ K 7 4
♣ J 4

West
♠ J 8
♥ Q J 10 8 2
♦ J 8
♣ 9 7 6 5

East
♠ Q 10 9 4
♥ 9 7
♦ Q 10 9 6 2
♣ A 8

South
♠ 5 2
♥ A 5 4
♦ A 5 3
♣ K Q 10 3 2

The bidding:

North	East	South	West
1 ♠	Pass	2 NT	Pass
3 NT	Pass	Pass	Pass

West opens the queen of hearts, and the dummy is put down. As always, you halt for a moment's thought.

You can surely win two top spades, two top hearts, and two top diamonds. Those cards will provide only six tricks, so you need three additional tricks for the contract.

Even at a glance you can see that the natural and logical way to develop three additional tricks is to establish the clubs. You have four high cards in clubs, and even if you use one of them to force out the ace, the other three will be good.

Having made your plan, you go ahead with it. You win the first trick with the ace of hearts. (It would be equally

24

correct to win the first trick with dummy's king of hearts.)

Your next step is to lead the deuce of clubs towards dummy's knave. If you had won the first trick in the dummy with the king of hearts, you next step would be to lead the knave of clubs from the dummy.

The reason for this play is that you must either win the trick in the *short* hand or at any rate use the *short* hand to force out the ace of clubs. It would be a mistake to use the king or queen or ten of clubs from the *long* hand on the first club trick.

East takes his ace of clubs, capturing dummy's knave. East leads back his nine of hearts, following the principle of defensive play that it usually pays the defenders to keep hammering away at a single suit. In this case West began the attack by leading a heart, and East continues the attack by leading another heart.

You can win this second heart with dummy's king. Then you lead dummy's four of clubs to your own king. Next you take the queen of clubs and then the ten of clubs. By this time you have led out four rounds of clubs, and West has had to follow suit each time. This exhausts all of his clubs, so that your three of clubs is the last club left. Hence you can lead the three of clubs and win a trick with it.

Having finished with the clubs, you can take the two top spades and the two top diamonds. You have taken ten tricks in all, making the contract with an over trick.

Before we go on to the next hand, let's learn a few lessons from this one. You developed some high-card tricks by the simple process of forcing out a higher card (the ace of clubs) held by the enemy. While you were taking your *high* clubs you happened to establish a *low* club, which gave you the over trick.

Most important of all, your first step was to develop the *new* tricks—not to cash the tricks that were lying about on surface. You would be defeated if you began the play by taking the top spades, the top hearts, and the top diamonds. You would *then* have to lead a club, and East would take the ace of clubs and would continue by taking three established diamonds and two established spades!

The art of playing the cards is to establish *your own* tricks without establishing tricks for the enemy. Your method is to force out the aces and kings held by the enemy and thus put yourself in position to cash your own high cards in those suits. Meanwhile, the enemy will be trying to force out *your* high cards. Don't do *their* work for them by needlessly cashing your aces and kings.

The Finesse

4.

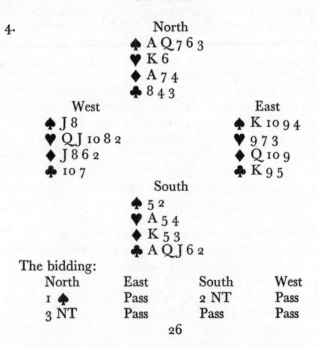

North
♠ A Q 7 6 3
♥ K 6
♦ A 7 4
♣ 8 4 3

West
♠ J 8
♥ Q J 10 8 2
♦ J 8 6 2
♣ 10 7

East
♠ K 10 9 4
♥ 9 7 3
♦ Q 10 9
♣ K 9 5

South
♠ 5 2
♥ A 5 4
♦ K 5 3
♣ A Q J 6 2

The bidding:

North	East	South	West
1 ♠	Pass	2 NT	Pass
3 NT	Pass	Pass	Pass

West opens the queen of hearts, and you look at the dummy and your own hand to plan the hand. You can count the following fast tricks: one spade, two hearts, two diamonds, and one club. The total is only six tricks, so you must look for a way to develop three additional tricks.

It's clear that you cannot develop extra tricks in the red suits, so you must choose between spades and clubs. You decide to try the clubs rather than the spades because of the greater strength of the club suit.

In order to develop the clubs you plan to lead the suit from the dummy towards your own hand and therefore you decide to win the first trick with dummy's king of hearts rather than with your own ace of hearts. (In the last hand it made no difference which hand won the first trick; this time there *is* a difference.)

After winning the first trick in dummy with the king of hearts you lead the three of clubs from dummy. East plays the five of clubs, and you *take a finesse* by playing the queen. Since East holds the king and West cannot beat your queen your finesse is successful.

Since you want to repeat the finesse, you must win a trick in dummy in order to lead clubs towards your hand again. Therefore you lead the three of diamonds from your hand and win the trick with dummy's ace of diamonds.

You may now lead from dummy, and you carry out your plan by leading the four of clubs towards your hand. East can do nothing to save himself. If he plays the king of clubs, you will capture it with your ace, after which your knave will be *high* (established); if East plays the nine of clubs you will finesse the knave, and this will win the trick since West cannot beat the knave.

East actually plays the nine of clubs, you play the knave, and West follows suit with the ten. You have now won two finesses, taking tricks with the queen and knave of clubs even though one of the opponents held a higher club (the king) all the time.

To add to East's unhappiness, you now lead the ace of clubs. He must follow suit with his king of clubs, and now your six and deuce of clubs are established. You promptly lead them, discarding low spades from the dummy.

You have now won one heart, one diamond, and five clubs. You can take the ace of spades, the ace of hearts, and the king of diamonds for a total of ten tricks. Before you do so, however, you can afford to try a finesse in spades.

You lead the deuce of spades from your hand, and West plays the eight of spades. You take a finesse by playing the queen of spades from dummy. As it happens, *this* finesse loses. East captures dummy's queen with the king of spades.

No harm has been done, however, since you can surely win the next trick no matter which suit East returns. You will then take your ten tricks and be content.

5.

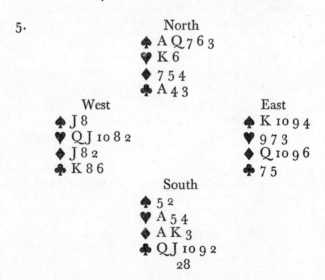

North
♠ A Q 7 6 3
♥ K 6
♦ 7 5 4
♣ A 4 3

West
♠ J 8
♥ Q J 10 8 2
♦ J 8 2
♣ K 8 6

East
♠ K 10 9 4
♥ 9 7 3
♦ Q 10 9 6
♣ 7 5

South
♠ 5 2
♥ A 5 4
♦ A K 3
♣ Q J 10 9 2

The bidding:

North	East	South	West
1 ♠	Pass	2 NT	Pass
3 NT	Pass	Pass	Pass

West opens the queen of hearts, and you pause to make your plan. You can count one fast trick in spades, two in hearts, two in diamonds, and one in clubs. The total is six tricks, and you therefore need three additional tricks for your contract.

Just as in the last hand, you decide to develop the clubs. This time, however, you must plan to lead clubs from your own hand towards the dummy. Hence you win the first heart trick with the ace in your own hand, rather than with dummy's king.

After you have won the first trick with the ace of hearts, you lead the queen of clubs towards the dummy. West plays the six of clubs, and you take a finesse by playing the three of clubs from the dummy.

East can play either the five or the seven of clubs, but he cannot beat your queen. Your finesse has succeeded.

You now repeat the finesse by leading the knave of clubs from your hand. If West plays low, you will play the low club from the dummy, and the finesse will succeed again. As it happens, West *covers* your knave of clubs with his king. You win the trick with dummy's ace.

Now you return dummy's remaining club, winning the trick with the ten of clubs in your own hand. The nine of clubs is, of course, high; and then the last club, the lowly deuce, will provide a fifth club trick.

When you have taken your five club tricks you are in position to take the ace of spades, the king of hearts, and the two top diamonds for a total of ten tricks. First, however, you can afford to try the spade finesse. You lead the low spade from your hand and finesse dummy's queen,

East wins with the king of spades, and your finesse has lost.

You are not worried, however, since you can win the next trick no matter which suit East returns. You will then, as in the last hand, take your ten tricks and be content.

We have now seen two different ways of finessing against a king. In one case you lead low cards, and in the second case you lead high cards. In both cases you lead towards the hand that holds the ace. If the second player puts up the king, you will be in position to win the trick with the ace; and if the second player plays low, you will be in position to finesse.

What happens if the second player doesn't have the king? Then the finesse fails—as in the case of the spade finesse in both of the preceding hands. Even then you are no worse off than if you hadn't tried the finesse.

Playing for a Drop

6.

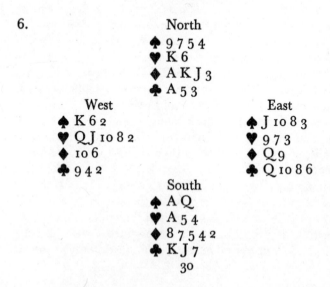

North
♠ 9 7 5 4
♥ K 6
♦ A K J 3
♣ A 5 3

West
♠ K 6 2
♥ Q J 10 8 2
♦ 10 6
♣ 9 4 2

East
♠ J 10 8 3
♥ 9 7 3
♦ Q 9
♣ Q 10 8 6

South
♠ A Q
♥ A 5 4
♦ 8 7 5 4 2
♣ K J 7

PLAY AT NO-TRUMPS

The bidding:

North	East	South	West
1 ♦	Pass	2 NT	Pass
3 NT	Pass	Pass	Pass

West opens the queen of hearts, and you follow your normal procedure. You count your tricks and make a plan before you play a single card from either hand.

You can win one fast trick in spades, two in hearts, two in diamonds, and two in clubs. Since the total is only seven tricks you must look for a way to develop two additional tricks.

You might think of developing one of those two tricks by means of a finesse in spades. As we shall see later on, there is a finesse in clubs also. If *both* finesses succeed, you will have your two additional tricks.

The odds on any finesse are even, but the odds are 3 to 1 against the success of *both* finesses. Let's look for a plan that has a better chance to succeed.

If you try to develop the diamonds, you have a very good chance to get four or five tricks in the suit instead of just the two top cards that you have counted. This plan will fail only if East has all four of the missing diamonds, and the odds are 20 to 1 against any such bad luck as that.

Obviously, it is better to adopt a plan with odds of 20 to 1 in your favour than another with odds of 3 to 1 against you. A shrewd bridge player plays *with* the odds rather than against them.

Having made your plan, you win the first trick with dummy's king of hearts. (It doesn't make much difference where you win the first heart trick.) Next you lead the ace of diamonds from the dummy. When both opponents follow suit, you can relax; your plan is sure to work.

You continue with the king of diamonds, and East has

to drop the queen in order to follow suit. You have played for the drop in diamonds, and your play has succeeded. The rest of the diamonds are established.

You are now in position to take five diamond tricks, a spade, two hearts, and two clubs, for a total of ten tricks. If you wish, you may take those tricks and go on to the next hand. It costs you nothing, however, to try for an extra trick or two by means of those finesses in clubs and spades that we mentioned before.

You therefore leave the diamonds temporarily, knowing that you can come back to them later on. You lead the three of clubs from the dummy. East plays the six of clubs, and you take a finesse by playing the knave. West cannot beat it, so your finesse succeeds.

This is a finesse against the queen. The other finesses that you have tried have been against the king of a suit.

You now return to the diamonds. You lead a low diamond to dummy's knave and return the three of diamonds from dummy, winning with the seven in your own hand. Next you lead your last diamond, the eight.

The time has come to try the spade finesse. First you must get to the dummy, so you lead the seven of clubs to dummy's ace. Next, you lead a low spade from the dummy. East plays a low spade, and you take a finesse by playing the queen. The finesse loses, for West wins with the king.

You have nothing to fear, however, since you can win the next trick no matter which suit West returns. You have kept the ace of spades, the ace of hearts, and the king of clubs in order to maintain control of the hand.

You take your eleven tricks quite happily. You needed only nine tricks for the contract, but you do not despise over-tricks.

Perhaps you noticed that a finesse was possible in diamonds. If you had wanted to do so, you could have led a low diamond from your hand with the intention of finessing dummy's knave. If West had the queen of diamonds, this finesse would succeed.

Why wasn't this finesse recommended? Not merely because the queen of diamonds happened to be in the *East* hand. In actual play you cannot tell in advance whether a finesse will win or lose.

The reason is that you should not finesse when a play for the drop is more likely to succeed. When the opponents have only four diamonds between them, you are more likely to catch the queen if you simply lead out the ace and the king than if you take a finesse. If the opponents had *five* diamonds between them, you would try a finesse, for then the odds would be against dropping the queen by playing the ace and the king.

You can remember this distinction by counting the number of cards that you and the dummy, combined, hold in a suit. If you have eight cards or fewer, take a finesse; if you have nine cards or more, play to drop the queen. (The old saying was: With eight, ever; with nine, never.)

MORE FINESSES

7.

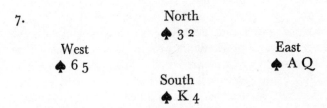

Your problem is to win a trick with the king of spades. Suppose, to begin with, that the lead is in the South hand. If you lead the king of spades, East will play the ace and will thus win the trick. East will also win the second spade trick with his queen.

Can you do any better by leading your *low* spade instead of the king of spades? No. When you lead your low spade, East will win the trick with his *queen*, thus saving the ace of spades to win a trick later on.

In short, you must surely lose both spade tricks if the lead is in the South hand.

The situation is different if the lead is in the *North* hand. You begin the suit by leading the deuce of spades.

If East plays his ace of spades, you are able to play the four of spades from the South hand. The next time spades are led, your king will win the trick.

If East plays the queen instead of the ace, you will play your king at the *first* trick. West will have to play a low spade, and your king will win at once.

As the cards lie, you are able to win a trick with your king of spades provided that you lead the suit first from the *North* hand. It doesn't matter whether East plays his ace on the first trick or on the second trick. Either way, your king will win a trick *when you lead towards it*.

Now let us exchange the East and West hands. This puts the ace-queen of spades in the *West* hand.

Whenever you play your king of spades, West will capture the trick with his ace. Whenever you play the low spade from your hand, West will be able to win the trick with the queen. This is equally true whether you lead from your own hand or from the North hand.

In short, you can win a spade trick if you lead the suit first from the North hand, provided that *East* has the ace. This will be true about half the time. Hence if you begin the suit correctly you have a fifty-fifty chance to win a trick in it.

8.

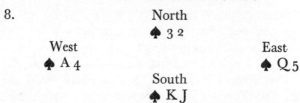

North
♠ 3 2

West
♠ A 4

East
♠ Q 5

South
♠ K J

South will not win any spade tricks if he begins the suit from his own hand. For example, if South begins by leading the king of spades, West will take the ace. This will leave East with the queen of spades, which will win the second spade trick.

South can gain nothing by leading the knave of spades from his hand to begin the suit. In this case, West will play low, and East will win the first trick with the queen of spades. Now West will be able to win the second spade trick with his ace.

As in all the previous examples, the correct play is to begin the suit with a lead from the North hand. *The general rule is to lead a suit from a weak holding towards a strong holding.*

When *North* begins the suit by leading the deuce of spades, East may play either the queen or the five.

If East plays the queen of spades, South can *cover* with the king of spades. South is now sure of a spade trick. If West takes the ace, South's knave will be good for the second spade trick. If West plays a low spade on the first trick, South wins that trick immediately with his king.

What happens if East plays the five of spades on the first trick of the suit? South must finesse the knave. If West wants to win the trick, he must play his ace. This will leave South in command of the suit with his king. If West does not play the ace, South's knave will win the first spade trick.

Now exchange the East and West hands. West now has the queen and five of spades, while East has the ace and four. South can still gain nothing by leading the suit from his own hand. Regardless of the position of the cards, the opponent who has the ace will take the trick whenever South leads the king; and the opponent who has the queen of spades will play it whenever South leads the knave. Either way, South must lose both tricks.

The proper procedure is still to lead the deuce of spades from the *North* hand at the first trick. East plays low, and South must decide whether to play the king or the knave.

When the cards are in their new position, South can win a spade trick only by playing the *king* at this moment. West will be obliged to play a low spade, and the king of spades will win.

If South tries to finesse the knave of spades, West will win with the queen of spades. Later on, East's ace of spades will win the other trick in the suit.

The question is: How does South know whether to play the *king* or the *knave* of spades at the first trick? The answer is that he *doesn't* know. He must guess!

Even a guess is better than nothing. No matter how unlucky South may be, he will sometimes guess right. When he does, he will win one spade trick. If South simply surrenders and leads the spades from his own hand, he will *never* win a spade trick.

You will meet many such 'guess' situations as you play bridge. Make your guesses quickly and get on with the game. The player who 'thinks' forever in such situations bores all the other players and doesn't really help his own chances.

9.

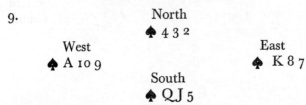

North
♠ 4 3 2

West
♠ A 10 9

East
♠ K 8 7

South
♠ Q J 5

The correct procedure is to lead the first spade from the North hand. East plays a low spade, and Souths play the queen. West must win with the ace since otherwise South would get a spade trick immediately with the queen.

In a complete hand West would now lead some other suit, and it would be important for North to win the trick in order to lead another spade. When the next spade is led, East may play either the king or the eight. If East plays the king, South plays the low spade and will have the knave of spades to win a spade trick later on. If East plays the eight of spades, South wins the trick immediately by playing the knave.

Notice that the situation is not changed if the East and West hands are exchanged. Notice also that South will lose all three spade tricks if he begins the suit by leading it from his own hand. (East will win the first trick in that case).

10.

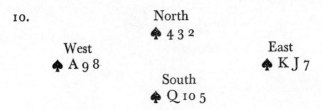

North
♠ 4 3 2

West
♠ A 9 8

East
♠ K J 7

South
♠ Q 10 5

The situation is very similiar to the last case. South can win a spade trick only by leading the suit twice from the North hand.

37

When North leads a low spade, South intends to play low if the king comes up; to finesse the ten if the small spade is played by East; or to play the queen if East puts up the knave. In any of these cases, South will have to get back to the North hand (by winning a trick in a different suit) in order to lead another spade towards his own hand. South will eventually win a spade trick.

11.

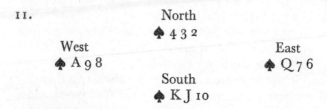

South must begin the suit by leading the deuce from the dummy. East plays low, and South finesses the knave. This play drives out West's ace.

Thus, the first finesse has succeeded. South can continue the process by winning a trick in another suit in the North hand. Then he leads another spade from dummy (North) through East's queen. If East plays low, South finesses the ten; if East puts up the queen, South's king wins and his ten is now good.

12.

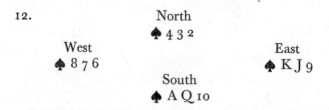

North leads the deuce of spades, and East's cards are trapped by the *double finesse*. If East plays the nine, South finesses the ten, winning the trick. South gets back to dummy in a different suit and leads another spade; and now South is in position to finesse the queen of spades. East cannot save himself by putting up the king or the knave of spades at the first trick; South will win the first trick as cheaply as possible and will later win a second finesse.

South must not finesse the queen of spades at the first trick if East plays the nine of spades. This would leave East with the king-knave of spades, and South with the ace-ten. There would be no further finesse, and East would surely win one spade trick.

Let's exchange the knave and the eight of spades, leaving the North and South hands untouched. When you finesse the ten of spades, you will lose to the knave. Later on, you will again lead a spade from the dummy and you will finesse the queen. The second finesse will succeed even though the first finesse lost.

Now try exchanging the *king* and the eight of spades. Now the first finesse of the ten of spades, drives out the king. This leaves you with the ace and queen in the South hand, and no further finesse is necessary.

There is still one remaining possibility. West may have both the king and the knave of spades. In this position both finesses lose, and you make only one spade trick (the ace).

You cannot tell in advance which finesses will win and which will lose. It usually costs you nothing to try the various finesses in the hope that some of them will succeed.

13.

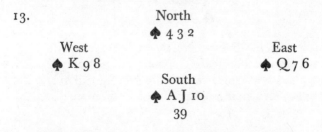

North
♠ 4 3 2

West
♠ K 9 8

East
♠ Q 7 6

South
♠ A J 10

Here we have a different example of the double finesse. South's problem is to win two out of the three spade tricks.

The suit is begun by a lead from the North hand. East plays low, and South finesses the knave. This drives out West's king. North must then regain the lead in a different suit and lead another spade. Now South is in position to finesse the ten of spades, thus winning two spade tricks.

The position would amount to the same thing if the East and West hands were exchanged. The finesse of the knave would then lose to the queen, but the second finesse (of the ten of spades) would succeed.

What happens if East has both the king and the queen of spades? He must play one of them at the first trick, since otherwise South wins the first trick by finessing the knave.

When East plays the queen of spades at the first trick, South wins with the ace. South can now afford to lead the knave of spades to drive out the king. The ten of spades will then be established—that is, it will be good to win the third spade trick.

What happens if *West* has both the king and the queen of spades? South then loses both of the finesses. He wins only one spade trick, with the ace.

14.

North
♠ 4 3 2

West
♠ 8 7 6

East
♠ Q J 9

South
♠ A K 10

Another double finesse. North leads a low spade, and East must decide whether to play low or to 'split his equals'. If East plays low, South wins a finesse immediately with the ten of spades, thus making sure of all three spade tricks.

If East splits his equals by putting up the knave, South wins with the king. South gets back to dummy and leads another low spade, trapping East's queen. If East plays low, South can finesse the ten; if East plays the queen, South wins with the ace and can cash his ten later on.

15.

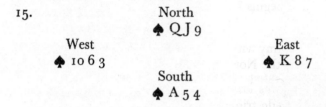

North
♠ Q J 9

West
♠ 10 6 3

East
♠ K 8 7

South
♠ A 5 4

You begin the suit by leading the queen from the North hand. East should play low, and you do too, allowing the queen to 'ride' for a finesse. The queen wins, and you have your ace to win a second spade trick.

You can win only two spade tricks against this correct defence. If you continue by leading the knave of spades from the North hand, East will cover with the king to drive out your ace; and this will set up West's ten for the third spade trick. If you continue at the second trick by leading the nine of spades from dummy, East plays low; and you must win with the ace to shut out West's ten. This leaves East with the king for the third spade trick.

Incorrect defence by East would enable you to win all three spade tricks! For example, East might mistakenly play the king of spades on the first trick when North leads the queen.

You then win with the ace of spades and lead a low spade back towards the dummy. Dummy's knave-nine then give you a finessing position over West's ten. For example, if West plays the six of spades on the second trick, North wins a finesse by playing the nine of spades.

The general rule for the defenders (East and West) is *not* to cover the queen when dummy also has the knave.

16.

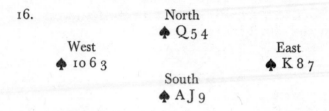

North
♠ Q 5 4

West
♠ 10 6 3

East
♠ K 8 7

South
♠ A J 9

If North begins by leading the queen, East must cover with the king. South wins with the ace of spades and returns to dummy with another suit in order to lead a second spade from the North hand. He now finesses the nine of spades, but this loses to West's ten. South therefore wins only two spade tricks.

South would win all three spade tricks against incorrect defence. For example, suppose that East fails to cover with the king when North begins the suit by leading the queen. The queen is allowed to ride as a finesse, winning the trick. Dummy is still in the lead, and immediately leads another spade. Now South can win a finesse with the knave, taking all three spade tricks.

The rule for the defenders in this case is *to cover the queen with the king when dummy does not also hold the knave.*

Let us repeat both of these rules because you will often meet these situations when you are defending. When dummy has *two or more honours in sequence*, you do *not* cover the first honour that is led through you for a finesse. When dummy has *only one honour*, however, and leads that honour through you for a finesse, you *do* cover.

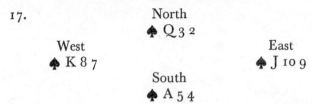

17.

North
♠ Q 3 2

West
♠ K 8 7

East
♠ J 10 9

South
♠ A 5 4

You must not begin the suit by leading the queen from the North hand. If you do, West wins that first trick with his king. You are no better off if the king of spades happens to be in the East hand. East covers the queen with his king of spades, driving out your ace. You cannot win a second spade trick.

The correct play is to take the ace of spades first and then lead a low spade towards North's queen. If West takes the king, North will win the third spade with the queen; and if West plays low, dummy's queen wins the second spade trick immediately.

You cannot be sure of winning a second spade trick. If the king of spades happens to be in the *East* hand, North's queen will not win a trick. The right play gives you a chance; the wrong play gives you no chance at all.

ENTRIES FOR FINESSES

Perhaps you have noticed that it is necessary to lead from a particular hand in order to take a finesse. You gain the right to lead by winning the preceding trick. A card that wins a trick and thus gives you the right to lead is called an 'entry'.

18.

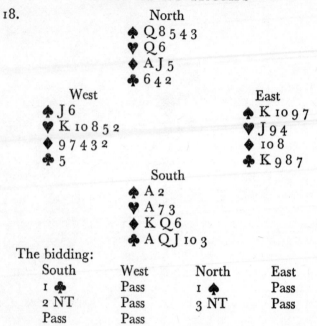

North
♠ Q 8 5 4 3
♥ Q 6
♦ A J 5
♣ 6 4 2

West
♠ J 6
♥ K 10 8 5 2
♦ 9 7 4 3 2
♣ 5

East
♠ K 10 9 7
♥ J 9 4
♦ 10 8
♣ K 9 8 7

South
♠ A 2
♥ A 7 3
♦ K Q 6
♣ A Q J 10 3

The bidding:

South	West	North	East
1 ♣	Pass	1 ♠	Pass
2 NT	Pass	3 NT	Pass
Pass	Pass		

West opens the five of hearts, and you stop to think. You can win one fast trick in spades, one in hearts, three in diamonds, and one in clubs. Since the total is only six tricks, you must look for a way to develop three additional tricks. The club suit is the obvious choice, and you therefore decide to take as many finesses as may be needed to establish the clubs.

But first you have a little problem about the first trick. You must put up dummy's queen of hearts in the hope that West has led from the king. The queen of hearts may win a trick at this moment, but it will never win a trick later on. Remember this position, because it happens quite often in actual play.

Fortunately for you, the queen of hearts does win the first trick. This gives you the right to lead a club from the dummy. Hence the queen of hearts is an entry.

East plays a low club, and you win with the queen. The finesse succeeds. You cannot be quite sure that the finesse has succeeded, because a crafty opponent will sometimes refuse the first trick that is offered to him in the hope that you will misjudge the situation and therefore misplay the hand.

In this case you have no problem. You want to get back to dummy as often as necessary in order to lead clubs. Your best course is to lead the six of diamonds from your hand and win in dummy with the knave of diamonds.

Now you can lead another club, finessing the knave from your own hand. West must discard, and now you have no further doubts about the club situation.

If you have counted the clubs carefully, you know that East still has the king and the nine. How do you count? You started with five clubs in your own hand and three in the dummy, eight in all. The opponents held the remaining five clubs. West could follow suit only once; hence East must have started with four clubs. East has played two of his four clubs, and must still have the other two of his original four clubs.

You must take another club finesse, and you must get to dummy to do so. Hence you lead the queen of diamonds and overtake with dummy's ace. This puts you in dummy and permits you to take a third club finesse—this time with the ten of clubs.

You can now lead out the ace of clubs, dropping East's king. Your three of clubs is now established, and you can cash it. You thus succeed in winning five clubs, three diamonds, two hearts, and a spade, a total of eleven tricks.

Note that the diamonds could be played in such a way as

to win two of the three tricks in the dummy—or two in your own hand. You happened to want entries to the *dummy*, so you won two tricks in dummy with the ace and knave. If you had wanted entries to your *own* hand, you would have won two diamond tricks in your own hand with the king and queen.

ENTRIES TO A LONG SUIT

19.

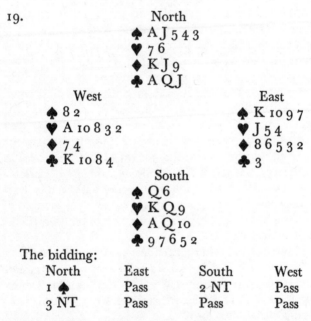

North
- ♠ A J 5 4 3
- ♥ 7 6
- ♦ K J 9
- ♣ A Q J

West
- ♠ 8 2
- ♥ A 10 8 3 2
- ♦ 7 4
- ♣ K 10 8 4

East
- ♠ K 10 9 7
- ♥ J 5 4
- ♦ 8 6 5 3 2
- ♣ 3

South
- ♠ Q 6
- ♥ K Q 9
- ♦ A Q 10
- ♣ 9 7 6 5 2

The bidding:

North	East	South	West
1 ♠	Pass	2 NT	Pass
3 NT	Pass	Pass	Pass

West opens the three of hearts, and you can count your tricks. You will make at least one heart, one spade, three diamonds, and one fast club trick. Since the total is only six tricks you must look for a way to develop three additional tricks.

The spade suit is stronger than it has been in most of the hands we have seen, but the club suit is still better. You must develop your additional tricks by taking club finesses and by establishing your long clubs. Having made your plan you play a low heart from the dummy. East plays the knave, and you take the queen.

You lead the deuce of clubs from your hand, West plays low, and you follow up your plan by finessing dummy's knave. East naturally plays his three of clubs, and your finesse succeeds.

You are going to need entries to your own hand this time, so you lead the nine of diamonds from the dummy and win with the ten of diamonds in your own hand. This puts you in position to lead another club from your own hand. You finesse dummy's queen, and East discards a diamond.

This is a blow, but not a serious one. You were hoping to win all five club tricks for an over-trick. (You would be able to do so if West had only *two* low clubs with his king. Two finesses and then the ace of clubs would exhaust West's clubs in that case, after which your last two clubs would be established.) Nevertheless, you go ahead with your plan since four club tricks will be enough for your contract and in the process you can afford to lose one trick.

After winning the second club finesse with dummy's queen you cash the ace of clubs. West follows suit, but still has the king of clubs left in his hand. You next lead the knave of diamonds from the dummy and win with the queen of diamonds in your hand. This permits you to lead a low club.

When all other methods of suit establishment fail, you must simply lead the suit and let the enemy take their tricks. In this case you must give West his king of clubs in order to establish your last club.

West returns the eight of spades, and you hastily put up dummy's ace. You must not risk the finesse. If you allowed East to win a spade trick, he would return a heart *through you*, and West would immediately take four heart tricks to defeat the contract!

This is a new principle. Sometimes you must *not* take a finesse. It is foolish to endanger your contract by finessing when you can make sure of your contract by refusing the finesse.

After taking the ace of spades you lead dummy's king of diamonds to your own ace of diamonds (notice that you have won all three diamond tricks in your own hand) and cash the good nine of clubs. This is your ninth trick.

Ducking

In the hand that you have just played you needed one entry in hearts and three in diamonds to develop the clubs. In the next hand your task is to make the long suit provide its own entries.

PLAY AT NO-TRUMPS

20.

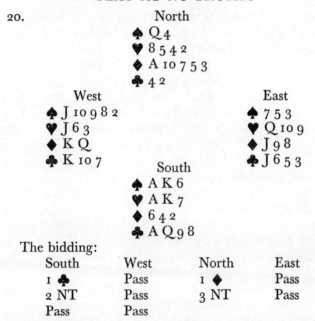

North
♠ Q 4
♥ 8 5 4 2
♦ A 10 7 5 3
♣ 4 2

West
♠ J 10 9 8 2
♥ J 6 3
♦ K Q
♣ K 10 7

East
♠ 7 5 3
♥ Q 10 9
♦ J 9 8
♣ J 6 5 3

South
♠ A K 6
♥ A K 7
♦ 6 4 2
♣ A Q 9 8

The bidding:

South	West	North	East
1 ♣	Pass	1 ♦	Pass
2 NT	Pass	3 NT	Pass
Pass	Pass		

West opens the knave of spades, and you count your tricks: three fast spades, two hearts, one diamond, and one club. Since the total is only seven tricks you must find a way to develop two additional tricks.

The diamonds are your best bet. The opponents have only five diamonds between them, which are probably divided 3-2—which means that one opponent has three diamonds and the other opponent has two.

Perhaps you haven't seen the importance of that 3-2 break in diamonds. It means that after three rounds of diamonds have been played, dummy's diamonds will be established because they'll be the only diamonds left. Dummy's fourth and fifth diamond will furnish the two tricks you are looking for.

One more fact to consider: You must not only establish dummy's long diamonds, but you must also eventually get back to dummy to cash them. Observe how this is done.

You win the first spade trick with the king in your own hand. If the opponents, when they 'get in' (win a trick), are foolish enough to leave the queen of spades in dummy, that card will eventually be the entry to your long diamonds. This is unlikely, for if the defenders play correctly they will lead a spade at the first opportunity, forcing the play of the queen before the diamonds are established—but it costs nothing to try!

You lead the deuce of diamonds from your hand, and West plays the queen. You must play a *low* diamond from the dummy! The purpose of this play, called 'ducking', will become clearer in a moment or two.

West wins the trick with his queen of diamonds and leads another spade. He is not foolish enough to let dummy keep the queen of spades until the diamonds have become established. You win in dummy with the queen of spades, but this entry is useless because you have been forced to use it too soon.

The ace of diamonds is the only other possible entry to the dummy, and you must take care not to use that card too soon. You have to lose another diamond trick in any case, and you must give it up while you still have a small diamond to return to dummy. Hence you now lead a *low* diamond from the dummy!

West wins with the king of diamonds and leads a third spade. You win with the ace of spades and lead your last diamond to dummy's ace. You are now in position to lead the fourth and fifth diamonds from dummy, assuring your contract.

After you have taken your diamonds, you must *not* try the club finesse. You must take your nine sure tricks: three spades, two hearts, three diamonds, and one club. If you try the club finesse it will lose, and West will take a total of five tricks: two spades, two diamonds, and one club.

You are willing to take finesses when they help you make your contract or when you are quite safe even if the finesse happens to lose. You do *not* take a finesse when that endangers an otherwise safe contract.

THE HOLD-UP

21

North
♠ 8 4
♥ J 8 4
♦ A Q J
♣ A Q 9 4 2

West
♠ K 10 6 5 2
♥ K 9 3
♦ 9 7 2
♣ 8 5

East
♠ Q J 7
♥ 10 7 6 2
♦ 10 8 5 4
♣ K 3

South
♠ A 9 3
♥ A Q 5
♦ K 6 3
♣ J 10 7 6

The bidding:

North	East	South	West
1 ♣	Pass	2 NT	Pass
3 NT	Pass	Pass	Pass

West opens the five of spades, and you count your tricks: one spade, one heart, three diamonds, and one club in top cards. Since the total is only six tricks you must find a way to develop three additional tricks.

Obviously you must establish the clubs, and this involves taking the finesse. The trouble is that although you can afford to lose one club trick, the opponents threaten to take four spades as well, which will defeat your contract before you can get properly started.

What can you do about it? You must interfere with West's entries to make it impossible for him to get all of his spade tricks. Or, to use a military expression, you must cut the communications between the two enemies.

You play a low spade from the dummy at the first trick, East plays the knave, and you play *low*. This refusal to win the trick is called a *holdup*. East now leads the queen of spades, and once more you hold up your ace of spades by playing your nine of spades. East continues with the seven of spades, and you are obliged to take your ace.

This simple play of holding up the ace of spades until the third round of the suit will make all the difference between making and losing the contract.

Now, you lead the knave of clubs from your hand, and when West plays low you let it ride for a finesse. East wins with the king of clubs, and must try to get to the West hand in order for West to cash his long spades.

How does East get to his partner's hand? East cannot lead a spade because he doesn't have any left in his hand. Your holdup exhausted East's spades—and this is exactly why you executed that play.

East leads the deuce of hearts, hoping that West can win the trick. You must *not* finesse. If you did, West would take the king of hearts and his good spades, setting you two tricks.

Instead you take the ace of hearts and proceed to cash the rest of the clubs and the top diamonds. You win nine tricks: one spade, one heart, three diamonds, and four clubs.

Note that you would have lost your contract if you had taken the first or second spade trick with your ace. East would have been able to lead a spade when he won his king of clubs, and then the opponents could take one club and four spades.

HOLD-UP WITH TWO STOPPERS

22.

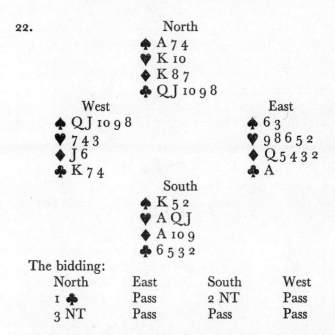

North
♠ A 7 4
♥ K 10
♦ K 8 7
♣ Q J 10 9 8

West
♠ Q J 10 9 8
♥ 7 4 3
♦ J 6
♣ K 7 4

East
♠ 6 3
♥ 9 8 6 5 2
♦ Q 5 4 3 2
♣ A

South
♠ K 5 2
♥ A Q J
♦ A 10 9
♣ 6 5 3 2

The bidding:

North	East	South	West
1 ♣	Pass	2 NT	Pass
3 NT	Pass	Pass	Pass

West leads the queen of spades, and you count your tricks: two spades, three hearts, and two diamonds. Since the total is only seven tricks you must develop two additional tricks.

Obviously you must establish the clubs. If you can force

out the ace and king, dummy's three remaining clubs will be good. In the meantime, however, the opponents threaten to establish their spades and to take three spades as well as two clubs. There is a race between the two black suits, and you must win the race.

Your method is to refuse the first trick. You must hold up even though you have two stoppers in the enemy's suit.

West continues with the knave of spades, and you win in your own hand with the king. (It doesn't really matter which hand takes the second trick, but you should get into the habit of keeping entries in both hands for the sake of flexibility.)

Next you lead a low club from your hand. West must not make the mistake of playing his king, for then his partner would have to capture the king with the singleton ace. West plays low, and East wins with the ace of clubs.

Since two rounds of spades have been played, East is out of spades. He can do you no harm. His best return is a heart, which you win in your own hand with the knave. Dummy still has the ace of spades to stop the dangerous spade suit, and you can afford to lead another club to drive out the king.

When you lead a second club, West can take his king. He has lost the race since his spades are not yet established, and your clubs are. West leads a spade to dummy's ace for lack of anything better to do.

Now you take the rest of the clubs and your top cards in the red suits. You win ten tricks: two spades, three hearts, two diamonds, and three clubs.

You would have lost your contract if you had won the first spade trick. When you then led clubs, East would have taken the ace of clubs and would have led his remaining spade. This would permit West to establish the rest of the spades, with the king of clubs still in his hand as the entry to the good spades.

What would you do if West held both the ace and the king of clubs? You would be defeated. As all bridge players discover, not every contract can be made even if you have bid and played correctly. If you wait for hands that cannot be lost no matter how the cards break you will have a long wait and the opponents will win thousands of points in the meantime by the simple process of bidding more aggressively than you do.

AVOIDANCE

Sometimes only one of the opponents is dangerous. In such a case you try to develop your tricks without allowing the dangerous opponent to gain the lead. This is called 'avoidance'.

23.

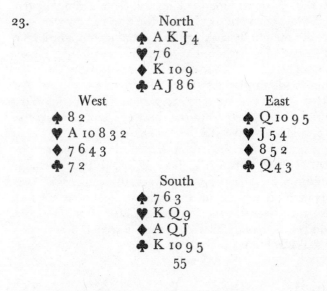

North
♠ A K J 4
♥ 7 6
♦ K 10 9
♣ A J 8 6

West
♠ 8 2
♥ A 10 8 3 2
♦ 7 6 4 3
♣ 7 2

East
♠ Q 10 9 5
♥ J 5 4
♦ 8 5 2
♣ Q 4 3

South
♠ 7 6 3
♥ K Q 9
♦ A Q J
♣ K 10 9 5

The bidding:

South	West	North	East
1 ♣	Pass	1 ♠	Pass
1 NT	Pass	3 ♣	Pass
3 NT	Pass	Pass	Pass

West opens the three of hearts, and you count your tricks: two spades, at least one heart, three diamonds, and two top clubs. Since the total is only eight tricks, you must look for a way to develop one additional trick.

The clubs are far better than the spades for this purpose. You can take two top clubs, give up a third trick in the suit and be sure of winning the fourth trick.

You may even do better than that. The clubs give you a chance for a 'two-way finesse'.

The queen of clubs is all that stands between you and four club tricks. If you think *West* has the queen, you can begin the suit by cashing the king and then leading the ten for a finesse. If you think *East* has the queen, however, you can begin the suit by cashing the ace and leading the knave for a finesse. The fact that you can finesse through either opponent at will, is what makes it a *two-way* finesse.

You decide to play for three club tricks one way or the other, and then you are ready to play to the first trick. You play the six of hearts from the dummy, East puts up the knave, and you win with the queen.

You must now realize that *East* is the dangerous opponent. If East wins a trick he will lead a heart through your king-nine. This will enable West to capture your two hearts with his ace-ten, after which West can take the rest of his hearts to defeat the contract. If *West* wins a trick, he can do you no harm; for if West leads a second heart, your king will surely take a trick.

Hence you must develop the clubs in such a way as to prevent East from winning a trick. That is very easy.

At the second trick you lead the five of clubs to dummy's ace. (You must *not* finesse dummy's knave on this first round of clubs, since that might allow East to win a trick.) At the third trick you lead the knave of clubs from the dummy. East plays a low club, and you allow the jack of clubs to ride for a finesse.

You hope that this finesse succeeds, to be sure, but you are safe even if it loses. If West has the queen of clubs (in an actual hand you wouldn't know which opponent held that card), he will be able to win the trick, but you are not afraid of any lead from West. *Your only concern is to avoid giving a trick to East.*

As it happens, the finesse succeeds. You continue with another club from dummy, and thus win all four club tricks. Now you can take your three diamonds and your two spades, making a total of ten tricks. You mustn't risk the spade finesse, of course, for that would allow the dangerous East player to gain the lead.

Ducking for Avoidance

24.

                    North
                    ♠ A K J 4
                    ♥ 7 6
                    ♦ K 10 9
                    ♣ A 6 3 2

West   East
♠ 8 2   ♠ Q 10 9 5
♥ Q 10 8 3 2   ♥ K 5 4
♦ 7 6 4 3   ♦ 8 5 2
♣ J 7   ♣ Q 9 8

                    South
                    ♠ 7 6 3
                    ♥ A J 9
                    ♦ A Q J
                    ♣ K 10 5 4

The bidding:

South	West	North	East
1 ♣	Pass	1 ♠	Pass
1 NT	Pass	3 ♣	Pass
3 NT	Pass	Pass	Pass

West opens the three of hearts, and you quickly see that
this is almost exactly the same as the previous hand. The
difference is that the clubs are weaker. You cannot *surely*
develop a third club trick without giving the lead to East.
Nevertheless you decide to make the attempt.

At the first trick you play a low heart from the dummy,
East puts up the king, and you win with the ace. Once
again, *East* is the dangerous opponent. The heart holding
is different, but the situation is the same. If East wins a
trick, he will lead a heart through you, and West will be

able to take four heart tricks. If *West* leads hearts, however, you have nothing to fear since your knave will surely win a trick. (Study the heart position in this hand and the preceding hand. They both occur frequently in actual play.)

After winning the first trick with the ace of hearts, you lead the four of clubs to dummy's ace. You next lead the deuce of clubs towards your hand. East plays the nine (he dares not play the queen since then your king would capture both the queen and the knave), and you finesse the ten of clubs.

You don't expect to win this finesse. It is actually as much a 'duck' as a finesse. You just want to give up one club trick to establish the rest of the suit; and you want to give up that trick to the non-dangerous opponent.

As the cards lie, the manœuvre succeeds. West wins with the knave of clubs. West dares not lead hearts again, since that would give you a second heart trick with your knave. Hence West shifts to the eight of spades.

You must *not* finesse dummy's knave. If you did, East would win with the queen of spades and return a heart. This would enable West to win four heart tricks, and you would be down two.

Instead, you go up with the king of spades. Your contract is safe without a finesse. You lead another club to your king, dropping East's queen on the way. Now the opponents are out of clubs, and you can safely lead a fourth round of clubs to win your third club trick.

That, plus two spades, one heart and three diamonds, gives you your contract.

You would have been in trouble if East's clubs had been queen-*knave*-eight. In that case you couldn't duck a club trick to West. East would play the eight of clubs when you led to dummy's ace, and would play the knave of clubs when you led the second club from dummy. If you won that trick with your king, East would be ready to win the third club trick with his queen.

CHOOSING THE SUIT TO ESTABLISH

Sometimes the process of developing tricks is simply a matter of giving the opponents what is rightfully theirs and thereby establishing the additional tricks that you need.

25.

North
♠ J 10 5
♥ A 8 4
♦ K J 9 6
♣ J 7 4

West
♠ A K
♥ Q 9 7 5 2
♦ 5 3
♣ Q 6 5 3

East
♠ 6 4 3 2
♥ 10 3
♦ Q 10 8 7
♣ 9 8 2

South
♠ Q 9 8 7
♥ K J 6
♦ A 4 2
♣ A K 10

The bidding:

South	West	North	East
1 NT	Pass	3 NT	Pass
Pass	Pass		

West opens the five of hearts, and you count your tricks: three hearts (the opening lead will give you a 'free' finesse), two diamonds, and two clubs in top cards. You need two additional tricks for your contract.

You might be able to obtain one or both of those tricks in diamonds. For example, you might take the ace of diamonds and then lead a low diamond from your hand to finesse either the nine or the knave. If that first finesse lost you might try a second finesse, or you might then play the king of diamonds in the hope of dropping the missing honour.

If no better plan turns up, you may go after the diamonds, but you look round for something better. The clubs offer you a chance to gain one additional trick. You might lead a club from the dummy and finesse the ten from your hand in the hope that East holds the queen.

You decide against a club finesse. For one thing, you need *two* tricks and you can't get excited about a plan that will bring in only *one* trick at best. More important, however, is the fact that you are looking for something surer than a mere finesse.

The spades are what the doctor ordered. You can give up two spades to the enemy and then you will surely be able to make the remaining two spades in your hand.

Before adopting the plan you check on what damage the enemy can do while you are developing the spades. You say to yourself (still before you have played a single card): 'If I win the first heart and lead a spade, the enemy will take the spade king and return a heart. I win and lead a spade to knock out the ace, and I can still win the heart return. Hence I am safe.'

Having considered everything you are now ready to play. You play low from the dummy, allowing the trick to come up to your king-knave. East plays the ten of hearts, and you win with the knave. You lead the seven of spades from your hand, and West takes the king of spades.

West returns the queen of hearts, and you win in dummy with the ace (or in your hand with the king). You lead another spade, and West takes his ace. West leads a third heart, which you win. Now you can take your tricks, winning, in all, two spades, three hearts, two diamonds, and two clubs.

This simple line of play brings the contract safely home. If you tried an early club or diamond finesse, however, you would lose your contract. For example, suppose you try a diamond finesse immediately after winning the first heart trick. East wins and returns a heart. Now West gets in with the king of spades to force out your last heart stopper; and West gets in again with the ace of spades to cash his two remaining hearts. The opponents win one diamond, two spades, and two hearts, defeating your game contract.

Perhaps you noticed two features of the last hand. The first is that the choice of the right suit to develop is sometimes a rather delicate matter. The second is that you must often judge the suitability of your own plans by noticing what damage the enemy can do in the meantime.

Establishing the Long Suit

26.

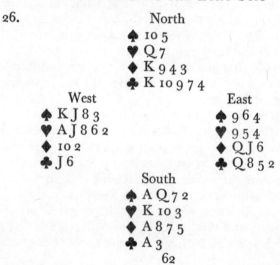

North
♠ 10 5
♥ Q 7
♦ K 9 4 3
♣ K 10 9 7 4

West
♠ K J 8 3
♥ A J 8 6 2
♦ 10 2
♣ J 6

East
♠ 9 6 4
♥ 9 5 4
♦ Q J 6
♣ Q 8 5 2

South
♠ A Q 7 2
♥ K 10 3
♦ A 8 7 5
♣ A 3

The bidding:

South	West	North	East
1 NT	Pass	2 NT	Pass
3 NT	Pass	Pass	Pass

West opens the six of hearts, and you count your tricks: one spade, two hearts (the opening lead will give you a 'free' finesse), two diamonds, and two clubs. Since the total is only seven tricks you must develop two additional tricks.

A successful finesse in spades would give you one additional trick. There is no chance of developing a long spade, since no possible break of the missing seven spades will leave you with the only spade. (The best break is 4-3, which means that one opponent has four spades—just as you do.) It would be foolish to go after the spades and set up a long spade for the enemy!

The diamonds are more promising. If the missing five diamonds split 3-2, which is normal and expected, you can develop one additional trick by taking the two top diamonds, giving up the third trick in the suit and then winning the fourth.

The trouble with this plan is that the opponent who wins the third round of diamonds will lead a heart, giving you your second heart trick. You will still have only eight tricks, and the opponents will be ready to run the hearts and defeat you the moment they gain the lead.

With this in mind you examine the last suit, clubs. You may be able to develop two additional club tricks by cashing the top clubs and giving up a club. This plan will work if each opponent has exactly three clubs or even if the clubs are 4-2 provided that the doubleton includes either the queen or the knave. Most important of all, if you play for the clubs you give up the lead *only once*.

With your mind made up, you play the seven of hearts

from the dummy at the first trick, allowing the trick to ride up to your king-ten. East plays the nine, and you win with the ten.

You next cash the ace of clubs and lead a low club towards dummy. West plays the knave, and you win with dummy's king. All is well now, since the clubs are sure to work out favourably. You continue by leading the *ten* of clubs from the dummy. (If you mistakenly led the seven of clubs from dummy, East would win with the eight and would later get the queen of clubs as well.)

East takes his queen of clubs, but cannot harm you. If East leads a heart, he will establish your second heart trick, and you will easily make two hearts, one spade, two diamonds, and four clubs. If East shifts to spades instead of returning a heart, you will play low. This will permit West to win a cheap trick with the knave, but will leave you quite safe against a spade continuation.

KNOCKING OUT THE DANGEROUS ENTRY

27.

North
♠ Q 6 5
♥ 9 8
♦ A K 7 3
♣ A Q 8 4

West
♠ A 9
♥ K 10 7 5 2
♦ 8 6 2
♣ 6 5 2

East
♠ 8 7 4 3
♥ J 6 4
♦ Q 10 9 4
♣ K 7

South
♠ K J 10 2
♥ A Q 3
♦ J 5
♣ J 10 9 3

The bidding:

North	East	South	West
1 ♦	Pass	1 ♠	Pass
2 ♣	Pass	2 NT	Pass
3 ♠	Pass	3 NT	Pass
Pass	Pass		

West opens the five of hearts, and you count your tricks: two hearts (since the opening lead gives you a free finesse), two diamonds, and one club in top cards. You need four additional tricks to make sure of your contract.

The black suits are the obvious sources of the four tricks. You can knock out the ace of spades and then take the other three spade tricks—but this leaves you one trick short. Well, then, you can try the club finesse instead. But even if the finesse succeeds, you will gain only three additional club tricks. (You will win four club tricks in all, but you have already counted the ace of clubs as one of your *fast* tricks.) You are still one trick short, even if the finesse works.

Reluctantly, you come to the conclusion that you must develop *both* black suits in order to make your contract. Which first?

Let's see what happens if you go after the *clubs* first. You play a low heart from the dummy, East puts up the knave, and you win with the queen. You lead the knave of clubs and let it ride for a finesse. East wins with the king of clubs and returns a heart.

You remember the hold-up play, so you refuse the second heart trick. (You couldn't refuse the first trick, for then you wouldn't win a trick with the queen of hearts.) Hearts are continued, and you must take your ace on the third round.

You now take the rest of the clubs and hopefully lead a spade. All will be well if *East* has the ace of spades, for East will be unable to lead a heart, thanks to your hold-up play. But luck is against you: *West* has the ace of spades, and he promptly takes it to defeat you with the rest of his established hearts. The defenders take one club, one spade, and three hearts.

Now let's go back to the first trick to see if you fare any better if you go after the *spades* first. You win the first trick with the queen of hearts and lead a low spade. West plays low, and dummy wins with the queen of spades. You lead another spade, and West must take his ace.

West leads the king of hearts, and you refuse the trick. West continues with the ten of hearts, and you must take your ace.

Now you cash your last two spades (discarding a low diamond from the dummy), and lead the knave of clubs for a finesse. East naturally wins with the king of clubs, but East can do no harm. He cannot return a heart, thanks to your hold-up play. The spades have already been played, and West's entry has already gone. East must return a club or a diamond. As a result, you win ten tricks: three spades, two hearts, two diamonds, and three clubs.

The principle is that you must force out the entry of the *dangerous* opponent before (not after) he has established his suit.

West is the dangerous opponent; he has led the long heart suit. If West has the king of clubs, it will *not* be an entry since your finesse will succeed whenever you try it. If West has the ace of spades it *will* be an entry, and you must therefore make West use his ace of spades before it is really useful to him—and before letting East use *his* entry—when it will be useless to your opponents.

MAKING THE ENEMY DISCARD

28.

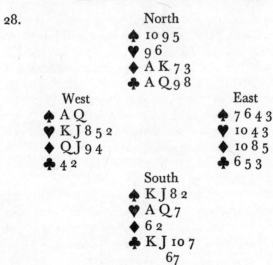

North
♠ 10 9 5
♥ 9 6
♦ A K 7 3
♣ A Q 9 8

West
♠ A Q
♥ K J 8 5 2
♦ Q J 9 4
♣ 4 2

East
♠ 7 6 4 3
♥ 10 4 3
♦ 10 8 5
♣ 6 5 3

South
♠ K J 8 2
♥ A Q 7
♦ 6 2
♣ K J 10 7

PLAY AT NO-TRUMPS

The bidding:

North	East	South	West
1 ♦	Pass	2 NT	Pass
3 NT	Pass	Pass	Pass

West opens the five of hearts, and you count your tricks: two hearts (since the opening lead gives you a free finesse), two diamonds, and four clubs. You need one additional trick.

The spade suit is the obvious source of your additional trick. Just to make sure, you check on what the opponents can do while you are developing your spade trick. You plan to enter dummy with a club (after winning the first heart trick), and lead the ten of spades. If East then plays the ace or the queen of spades, you will have no problem; all you need is *one* spade trick. If East plays low, you will try to guess whether to play the king or the knave.

For the sake of argument, let's suppose that you guess wrong or that West has both the ace and the queen of spades. (This is actually the case, but you wouldn't know if if you were playing an actual hand.) West will have two sure spade tricks, no matter how you play the spades. He will take his first spade and force out your second heart stopper. Later, West will take his second spade trick and cash his established hearts to defeat the contract. West will get, in all, two spades and three hearts.

What can you do to guard against this danger? You can create a problem for the defenders by running your four club tricks before you do anything about the spades. Let's go back to the first trick and see how it works out.

You play a low heart from the dummy, East covers with the ten of hearts, and you win the first trick with the queen. You next cash the king of clubs, followed by the knave of clubs. Next, you lead a third club to the dummy.

68

When the third round of clubs is led, West must discard. What does he throw away?

Obviously West cannot afford to throw away one of his good spades. Can West throw a low diamond? If he does, you will cash the two top diamonds and give up one diamond, after which dummy's last diamond will be established. West must keep all of his diamonds to prevent you from establishing a long diamond in the dummy.

If West cannot throw a spade or a diamond, he must discard a heart. Nothing else is left. But the moment West throws a heart you are quite safe. You can afford to give West two spades and *two* hearts; you couldn't afford to give him *three* hearts.

To make doubly sure, you lead out dummy's ace of clubs, thus forcing West to discard again. This time both opponents must discard, and you may gain information from East as well as from West.

In any case, you can then afford to lead the ten of spades from dummy. West takes a spade trick and forces out your ace of hearts. You give up a second spade trick, and West takes two heart tricks. There the defenders come to a halt: you have the rest of the tricks.

What would you do if the diamonds and clubs in the East and West hands were exchanged? Then West would have three worthless diamonds and three worthless clubs. He would have to make only one discard on the clubs, and could easily spare one of his worthless diamonds.

You would then have to fall back on the spades. If those worked out badly, as they would in this case, you would be defeated. Too bad, of course, but don't waste any tears over it. You must get used to the idea that some hands *cannot* be made no matter how skilfully you play them.

Perhaps you have a different complaint. You have been told to begin the play of a hand by developing *new* tricks instead of taking your *sure* tricks. Yet in this hand you are advised to cash all the clubs before tackling the spades.

The reason it is correct to cash the clubs in this case is that this play *doesn't establish any tricks for the opponents*. It is unwise to begin by cashing your scattered top cards, because that will usually set up tricks for the enemy. There is no such danger to be feared when you have a long, *solid* suit. You can afford to run it in the hope that the opponents will make things easier for you by their discards.

THREE

Play at a Trump Contract

You are now ready to learn something about the play of the hand at a trump (suit) contract. Everything that you have learned so far will be useful to you. As declarer at a suit contract you will use all the weapons that you have learned to use at no-trumps—and a few others besides.

As we have seen, the big danger at a no-trump contract is the enemy's long suit. This is far less dangerous at a suit contract, for your trump suit usually acts as a rampart to stop the enemy's suit. Sometimes your own trumps will protect you, and sometimes dummy's trumps will do the job.

At a no-trump contract, each suit has to stand or fall by itself. At a suit contract, however, you can use your trumps (or dummy's trumps) to help in the job of establishing a side suit.

At a no-trump contract, if you have five clubs in the dummy and four clubs in your own hand, you can win five clubs at most. At a trump contract you can sometimes win all your trumps *separately*. If clubs were trumps in such a hand, you might win *nine* tricks with those clubs!

Sometimes your general line of play at a suit contract is to draw trumps fairly early and then develop your other tricks. At other times your plan is to ruff one suit in the dummy and another suit in your own hand (*a cross-ruff*), thus making most or all of your trumps separately. When you plan a partial or complete cross-ruff you avoid drawing trumps.

One more general remark: as always, you study the dummy and plan your play before actually playing. You have learned to begin the planning of a no-trump hand by counting your winners. At a suit contract you usually *count losers* instead of winners. If you plan to ruff often in your own hand, however, you go back to the no-trump practice of counting your *winners*.

DECLARER'S TRUMPS AS STOPPERS

29.

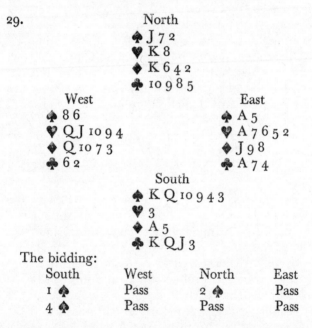

North
♠ J 7 2
♥ K 8
♦ K 6 4 2
♣ 10 9 8 5

West
♠ 8 6
♥ Q J 10 9 4
♦ Q 10 7 3
♣ 6 2

East
♠ A 5
♥ A 7 6 5 2
♦ J 9 8
♣ A 7 4

South
♠ K Q 10 9 4 3
♥ 3
♦ A 5
♣ K Q J 3

The bidding:

South	West	North	East
1 ♠	Pass	2 ♠	Pass
4 ♠	Pass	Pass	Pass

West leads the queen of hearts, and you count your

losers: one trump loser, one in hearts, none in diamonds, and one in clubs. The total is three losers.

The hand presents no problem, but you must still learn how to go through the correct motions. You will eventually play hands of this sort without any thought at all, but you will have to think the first few times.

You play the king of hearts from the dummy at the first trick. You don't really expect the king to win the trick, because only a very foolish opponent would be leading the queen of hearts against a suit contract if he also had the ace of hearts; but the king certainly won't do you any good later on.

East wins with the ace of hearts and returns a heart. You trump with the three of spades, winning the trick. Your trump suit has protected you from the enemy's long heart suit. If you had been playing this hand at no-trumps, the opponents would have taken five hearts and two other aces.

You lead the king of trumps, forcing out the ace. East returns the four of clubs (hoping that his partner has the king—or even the queen). You put up the king of clubs, winning the trick. You now lead the queen of trumps.

By this time you have exhausted the trumps held by the opponents. How do you know? You counted six trumps in your own hand and three in dummy, leaving four to be divided between the opponents. You have seen both opponents follow suit on two rounds of trumps, so you know without consciously counting to thirteen that all the trumps must now be drawn.

Having drawn the trumps you now lead a club to force out the ace. You will then be able to cash the other club tricks, knowing that the opponents cannot trump when they run out of clubs. You have used your own small trumps against the enemy's long heart suit, and you draw trumps to prevent them from using their small trumps against your long club suit.

You eventually take your top diamonds, and thus you have made your contract.

DUMMY'S TRUMPS AS STOPPERS

30.

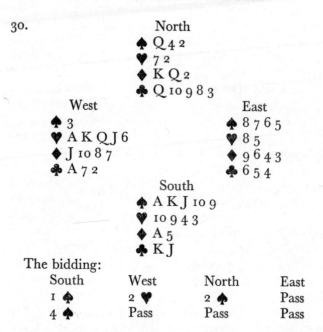

North
♠ Q 4 2
♥ 7 2
♦ K Q 2
♣ Q 10 9 8 3

West
♠ 3
♥ A K Q J 6
♦ J 10 8 7
♣ A 7 2

East
♠ 8 7 6 5
♥ 8 5
♦ 9 6 4 3
♣ 6 5 4

South
♠ A K J 10 9
♥ 10 9 4 3
♦ A 5
♣ K J

The bidding:

South	West	North	East
1 ♠	2 ♥	2 ♠	Pass
4 ♠	Pass	Pass	Pass

West opens the king of hearts, and you count your losers: none in trumps, two fast losers in hearts, none in diamonds, and one in clubs. You will have to decide what to do about your other two losers in hearts.

Perhaps you can ruff your third and fourth hearts in the dummy. Then again, you can discard one of them on dummy's extra high diamond. If the opponents are obliging, perhaps you will be able to get discards on dummy's clubs.

You make a mental note of these various possibilities and decide to play a few tricks and see what happens. On West's king of hearts you play a low heart from the dummy, and East plays the *eight* of hearts. West now leads the knave of hearts, you play dummy's remaining heart, and East follows suit with the *five* of hearts.

Why has East played the eight of hearts first and the five of hearts next? This 'high-low' is a signal, asking West to lead the suit again.

Why would East want the suit led again? East cannot have high hearts because West has bid and played the suit in such a way as to show all the top cards. East must be signalling a doubleton, which means that he is ready to ruff the third round.

West now leads the queen of hearts. You must ruff in dummy to avoid losing the trick. What's more, you must ruff with dummy's *queen* of trumps since otherwise East will over-ruff and thus take the trick away from you.

When you ruff the third heart with dummy's queen, East discards a low diamond. You now know that you have correctly read East's signal, and you congratulate yourself on ruffing *high* in the dummy to shut out an over-ruff.

Your next step is to draw trumps. You cannot safely ruff any more hearts in the dummy, so you might just as well get the trumps out. You lead a low trump from dummy to your ace and then continue with the king. West discards on the second trump, so you realize that you will have to lead out *four* rounds of trumps to draw them all.

After you have drawn four rounds of trumps (discarding low clubs from the dummy), you prepare to discard your last heart. You cash the ace of diamonds and then lead the low diamond to dummy's king. Next you lead the queen of diamonds from the dummy, discarding the last heart from your hand.

This 'discard' is a play that we didn't bother with in the play at no-trump. The reason is that a discard at no-trumps doesn't add to your winners or subtract from your losers. At a suit contract, however, the discard puts you in position to trump when the suit (hearts, in this case) is led again. Thus you have disposed of a loser.

You can now turn your attention to the clubs. You lead a low club from the dummy and play the king from your hand. West can take his ace, but if he plays a heart—or a diamond—you can trump. You easily win the last two tricks with the last trump and a high club.

In this hand, *dummy's* trumps protected you against the enemy's long suit. You saw a defensive signal and acted against it. And, finally, you discarded a loser of one suit (hearts) on another suit (diamonds) so that you could trump hearts later.

ESTABLISHMENT BY RUFFING

31.

	North		
	♠ J 9 8 4		
	♥ 9 5		
	♦ 7		
	♣ A K 10 6 5 2		

West		East	
♠ 6 5		♠ 10 7	
♥ Q 10 6 4 3		♥ K J 8	
♦ A 9 8 5		♦ K J 6 4 2	
♣ 7 4		♣ Q J 9	

	South		
	♠ A K Q 3 2		
	♥ A 7 2		
	♦ Q 10 3		
	♣ 8 3		

The bidding:

South	West	North	East
1 ♠	Pass	2 ♣	Pass
2 ♠	Pass	3 ♣	Pass
4 ♠	Pass	Pass	Pass

West opens the four of hearts, and you count your losers: none in trumps, one in hearts, one fast loser in diamonds, and none in clubs.

The trouble with this particular hand is that it won't work out quite that way. If you try to ruff two diamonds and one heart in the dummy, the opponents will get the lead once in hearts and once in diamonds. They can lead trumps each time, thus taking two of the four trumps out of the dummy. You can't ruff three cards with only two trumps. Moreover, even if the opponents didn't lead

77

trumps, you'd have trouble getting back to your hand after you had ruffed each time in the dummy.

What to do? There is a standard method of playing a hand of this sort. Whenever dummy has a long, strong suit and a good supply of trumps you plan to establish this long suit (rather than to play for a ruff or two in the dummy).

Let's see how it works out. On West's lead you play a low heart from the dummy, East puts up the king, and you win with the ace. You lead the ace and then the king of trumps, drawing all four trumps held by the enemy. You draw trumps quite early when you intend to establish and cash a long suit.

You next step is to take the ace and king of clubs. The opponents have only five clubs between them, and when they both follow suit twice, you know that the break is 3-2. You can now ruff one of dummy's low clubs, and all three of dummy's remaining clubs are established.

This is a play that you cannot execute at no-trumps. You have used your trump suit to help establish the clubs.

You can get three discards on dummy's cluds. It is true that you could now fulfill your contract by leading a heart or a diamond, thus allowing the enemy to take one trick in each red suit. Then you could ruff the return of either a heart or diamond in the dummy and play out the long clubs, discarding your other losers.

Because of the lucky breaks in both black suits, however, you now discover that there is no need to lose *two* tricks. You can lead your three of trumps to dummy's knave and obtain three fast discards on dummy's three established clubs. You will be careful to throw your two low *hearts* and only one of the diamonds. (Reducing to a singleton diamond in your hand would be no advantage, since dummy already has a singleton.) Next you will give up one diamond and ruff your last diamond with dummy's last trump. Now all your cards are high.

THE RUFFING FINESSE

32.

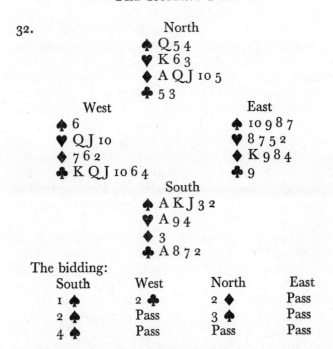

North
♠ Q 5 4
♥ K 6 3
♦ A Q J 10 5
♣ 5 3

West
♠ 6
♥ Q J 10
♦ 7 6 2
♣ K Q J 10 6 4

East
♠ 10 9 8 7
♥ 8 7 5 2
♦ K 9 8 4
♣ 9

South
♠ A K J 3 2
♥ A 9 4
♦ 3
♣ A 8 7 2

The bidding:

South	West	North	East
1 ♠	2 ♣	2 ♦	Pass
2 ♠	Pass	3 ♠	Pass
4 ♠	Pass	Pass	Pass

West opens the king of clubs, and you count your losers: none in trumps, one in hearts, none in diamonds, and up to three losers in clubs. Your plan is to develop the diamonds in order to dispose of some of your excess losers.

Why don't you plan to ruff some of your low clubs in the dummy? The trouble with that idea is that East is sure to be short in clubs also, and he will be delighted to over-ruff the dummy. How do you know that East is short in clubs? Since West has bid the suit, he should have five or six clubs. You can see six clubs between your own hand and the dummy. There are only thirteen clubs altogether, so East cannot have more than one or two cards in the suit.

Sometimes this kind of information doesn't particularly help you, but it never hurts you. Sometimes you get so many clues from the enemy's bids and plays that you can play the whole hand as though all the cards were face up on the table!

Let's proceed with the play, because you're about to be shown something new. You play a low club from the dummy, East plays the nine, and you win with the ace.

Your next step is to draw trumps. You lead a low trump to dummy's queen and return a low trump from dummy to your ace. West discards a club, so you know that the five trumps held by the enemy are split 4-1. You must draw two more rounds of trumps. (Dummy discards a heart on the fourth trump.)

Now comes the new play. You lead a diamond to dummy's ace and return the queen of diamonds. If East plays the king of diamonds you will trump and get back to dummy with the king of hearts to run the rest of the diamonds. If East plays a low diamond instead of the king, you will discard one of your losing clubs. The queen of diamonds will win the trick, and you will be in position to continue the finesse with dummy's *knave* of diamonds.

What if *West* happens to have the king of diamonds? He wins the trick with it. Any finesse can lose, and this type is no exception.

If West does win that trick, he gets one of your losing clubs on it. He can collect two more club tricks, but then he is through. You can ruff a club continuation, get back to dummy with the king of hearts, and discard your losing heart on the knave of diamonds. You will still make your game contract.

Note that you would risk the loss of the contract if you made the mistake of discarding a low *heart* on the queen of diamonds. If West happened to win that trick, he could then cash three club tricks for a total of four defensive tricks.

As it happens, *East* has the king of diamonds, and the queen of diamonds holds. You continue with the knave of diamonds next, and trump whenever East puts up his king. You then get back to dummy with the king of hearts to discard on the rest of dummy's diamonds. You win twelve tricks in all.

Note also that you couldn't ruff out the king of diamonds by leading *low* diamonds from the dummy and ruffing in your own hand. It was essential to lead a *high* diamond from the dummy so that, if West held the king, only that card could be lost and the other diamonds in dummy would be winners.

RUFFERS IN THE DUMMY

33.

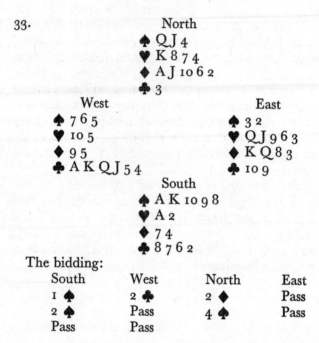

North
♠ Q J 4
♥ K 8 7 4
♦ A J 10 6 2
♣ 3

West
♠ 7 6 5
♥ 10 5
♦ 9 5
♣ A K Q J 5 4

East
♠ 3 2
♥ Q J 9 6 3
♦ K Q 8 3
♣ 10 9

South
♠ A K 10 9 8
♥ A 2
♦ 7 4
♣ 8 7 6 2

The bidding:

South	West	North	East
1 ♠	2 ♣	2 ♦	Pass
2 ♠	Pass	4 ♠	Pass
Pass	Pass		

West opens the king of clubs, and you count your losers: none in trumps, none in hearts, one in diamonds, and from one to four in clubs. You must plan to reduce the number of losers in some way.

Is there a long establishable suit on which you can discard your losers? The diamonds are the only hope, and they are not particularly long or strong. You must make do with this kind of suit if no better plan presents itself, but let's look for something better.

Can you ruff out enough losers? Yes, if the opponents are

accommodating enough. You can ruff all the rest of your clubs with dummy's three trumps, and you can return to your hand by the ace of hearts and (later) heart ruffs.

Having made your plan, you follow suit at the first trick with dummy's singleton club. East plays the nine of clubs, and you play the deuce.

West now leads the seven of spades. He sees that you plan to ruff losing clubs in the dummy, and leads a trump to reduce dummy's ruffing power. How does West know what you have in mind? He can see the singleton club and the three trumps in the dummy and he can guess the rest.

Where should you win this trump trick? In your own hand, because you want to lead a club and ruff it in the dummy. You do both of these things and return to your hand with the ace of hearts. This permits you to ruff another club with dummy's last trump.

Note that you have been able to ruff only two of your clubs in the dummy. West's shrewd trump lead cost you a trick. Note also that you ruffed out two clubs without giving up the lead, because you didn't want to give the enemy a chance to lead *another* trump.

The rest of the hand is very easy. Your safest course is to draw the rest of the trumps, but to do so you must get back to your hand. You cash dummy's king of hearts, lead a third heart which you ruff in your hand, and then draw two rounds of trumps. Now it is safe to lead a diamond from your hand and finesse dummy's ten. East wins with the queen of diamonds and returns a heart, forcing you to ruff.

At this moment you have already won nine tricks, and you now have a low diamond and a low club. Lead your diamond to dummy's ace and collect your tenth trick. Don't risk the contract with any more finesses.

PLAY AT A TRUMP CONTRACT

DISCARDS IN THE DUMMY

We have already seen how you may reduce the number of losers by discarding on dummy's long suit. This idea works in reverse, too: you can discard from the dummy on your own long (or long*er*) suit.

34.

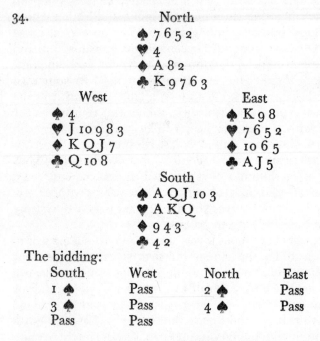

North
♠ 7 6 5 2
♥ 4
♦ A 8 2
♣ K 9 7 6 3

West
♠ 4
♥ J 10 9 8 3
♦ K Q J 7
♣ Q 10 8

East
♠ K 9 8
♥ 7 6 5 2
♦ 10 6 5
♣ A J 5

South
♠ A Q J 10 3
♥ A K Q
♦ 9 4 3
♣ 4 2

The bidding:

South	West	North	East
1 ♠	Pass	2 ♠	Pass
3 ♠	Pass	4 ♠	Pass
Pass	Pass		

West opens the king of diamonds, and you count your losers: possibly one in spades (the king is out against you), none in hearts, two in diamonds, possibly two in clubs. Too many!

What can you do to reduce the number of losers? Is there a long suit, on which you can get discards?

Take a look at the heart suit. It isn't very long, but it's solid—and two cards longer than dummy's heart suit! You win the first trick in dummy with the ace of diamonds. Then you lead a heart to your ace. You lead the king of hearts, discarding one of dummy's losing diamonds. Then you lead the queen of hearts and discard dummy's other losing diamond.

This puts you in position to ruff your losing diamonds in the dummy. What's more, each ruffing trick will give you an entry to the dummy. What do you need those entries for? You have to finesse for that king of trumps, remember?

After running your three hearts, you lead a low diamond and ruff it in the dummy with the deuce of spades. You next lead the five of spades from dummy and finesse the queen of spades from your hand. It wins the trick.

You continue the process. You lead your last low diamond and ruff it in dummy with the six of trumps. Then you lead the seven of trumps from the dummy and finesse the knave of spades. That finesse also succeeds. Now you can lead out the ace of trumps, dropping East's king.

You have disposed of all of the losers except the clubs. Can you do anything about them? All you can do is lead towards dummy's king in the hope that West has the ace. If so, you will lose only one club trick; otherwise you will lose two.

As it happens, *East* has the ace, and you lose two club tricks. You are well satisfied, however. You have made your contract with an over-trick.

Perhaps you wonder why there was such a hurry to lead the hearts. Why not take a trump finesse first? It wasn't safe. If the trump finesse had lost at the second trick, West would have taken two diamond tricks at once. You had to get rid of the losers first. When you finally took the trump finesse, you were quite safe even if it happened to lose.

PLAY AT A TRUMP CONTRACT

TRUMPS FOR COMMUNICATION

As you have already seen it is important to lead from a particular hand if you want to develop a suit to best advantage. If you happen to get to the wrong hand, you must find a way to get yourself into the right hand before you resume your plan. Cards that take you from one hand to another are called cards of *communication*.

Any suit may provide you with communication, and the trump suit is no exception. When the trumps are needed for this purpose, you may have to postpone the drawing of trumps until the need for communication has passed.

35.

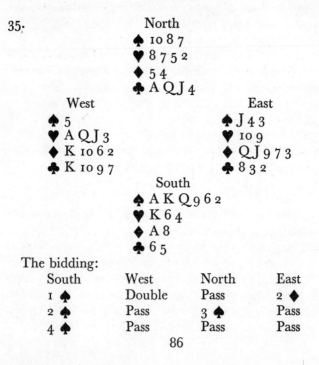

North
♠ 10 8 7
♥ 8 7 5 2
♦ 5 4
♣ A Q J 4

West
♠ 5
♥ A Q J 3
♦ K 10 6 2
♣ K 10 9 7

East
♠ J 4 3
♥ 10 9
♦ Q J 9 7 3
♣ 8 3 2

South
♠ A K Q 9 6 2
♥ K 6 4
♦ A 8
♣ 6 5

The bidding:

South	West	North	East
1 ♠	Double	Pass	2 ♦
2 ♠	Pass	3 ♠	Pass
4 ♠	Pass	Pass	Pass

West opens the deuce of diamonds and you count your losers: none in trumps (unless West has all four of the missing trumps, which is very unlikely), perhaps three in hearts, one in diamonds, and perhaps one in clubs. Since the total may run as high as five losers, you must do something to reduce the loss.

A successful finesse in clubs will prevent the loss of a club trick. What's more, if you repeat the finesse, you will get three club tricks and will be able to discard a loser on the dummy's third high club. This will reduce the count of losers from five to three, which is just what you can afford.

Let's go ahead with the plan and see what happens. You play a low diamond from the dummy, East puts up the knave, and you win with the ace. You draw two rounds of trumps with the ace and king, discovering that East still has a third trump.

Should you draw that last trump? Let's suppose first that you do. You lead the queen of spades, removing the last trump from the East hand—and also from the dummy.

Now you lead a club from your hand and finesse dummy's knave of clubs. The finesse succeeds, and you are in the dummy. How do you get back to your hand to repeat the finesse? If you lead a diamond or a heart, the opponents will take three hearts and a diamond. If you lead clubs, you will not be able to repeat the finesse. You are stuck in the wrong hand, with no way out.

You are much better off if you don't draw East's last trump. Draw just *two* rounds of trumps, and then finesse the knave of clubs. When the finesse succeeds you can get out of dummy by leading the third trump to your queen. This not only draws East's last trump but also gets you safely into your own hand. One result is just as important as the other.

Now that you are back in your hand, you can lead the

six of clubs towards the dummy. West plays low, and you must finesse dummy's queen of clubs even though this is your last club. In for a penny, in for a pound!

The finesse succeeds again, as you expected, and you can now lead the ace of clubs from the dummy and discard the losing diamond on it. No matter what happens from now on, you cannot lose more than the three heart tricks.

This is your only chance to get a heart trick, so you lead a heart from dummy towards your king. You will make an over-trick if East happens to have the ace of hearts. As it happens, your king is captured by West, and the defenders speedily take three heart tricks. You then win the rest with trumps, making your contract.

The Cross-ruff

Sometimes the easiest way to make your contract is to make your trumps separately, ruffing one suit in the dummy and another suit in your own hand. This is called a cross-ruff.

36.

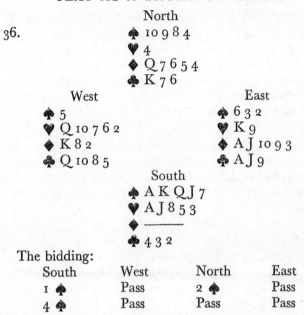

North
♠ 10 9 8 4
♥ 4
♦ Q 7 6 5 4
♣ K 7 6

West
♠ 5
♥ Q 10 7 6 2
♦ K 8 2
♣ Q 10 8 5

East
♠ 6 3 2
♥ K 9
♦ A J 10 9 3
♣ A J 9

South
♠ A K Q J 7
♥ A J 8 5 3
♦ —
♣ 4 3 2

The bidding:

South	West	North	East
1 ♠	Pass	2 ♠	Pass
4 ♠	Pass	Pass	Pass

West opens the six of hearts, and you count your losers: none in trumps, none in diamonds, perhaps three in clubs. The hearts have not been counted because the number of heart losers depends on how you play the hand. If you draw trumps, you will probably lose one or two hearts—perhaps more. If you ruff all four of your small hearts in the dummy, you won't lose *any* hearts.

This is a hand in which you plan to do some substantial ruffing in your own hand, so you must count *winners* instead of losers. You will ruff four hearts in the dummy, returning to your own hand each time by ruffing diamonds. This will allow you to win all nine of your trumps separately. The ace of hearts will provide a tenth trick. Ten tricks are enough for your contract, so you adopt the plan.

You play a low heart from the dummy, East puts up the king, and you win with the ace. You lead a low heart from your hand and ruff with the four of spades in the dummy. East follows suit, and you relax.

What were you worried about? This is the only trump that can possibly be over-ruffed. From now on you will be ruffing with *high* trumps, so there will be no danger of an over-ruff.

It wouldn't have done you any good to ruff that first heart with the eight of spades. You're going to have to ruff hearts *four* times, so you'll have to use the four of spades sooner or later. It's better to use it early, because then there is an excellent chance that East will have to follow suit and will not be able to think about over-ruffing. If you use the four of spades *later*, however, there is a far greater danger that East will have used up all of his hearts, and will therefore be able to over-ruff. This is a general principle of ruffing—use the low trumps early, and save the high trumps for later.

You return a low diamond from the dummy and ruff in your own hand. And you just continue that way, ruffing hearts in the dummy and diamonds in your own hand. You make nine trump tricks and the ace of hearts, fulfilling your contract.

It's worth noting that West could have defeated the contract by leading a trump instead of the six of hearts at the very first trick. This would have removed one of the trumps from the dummy, limiting you to *eight* trump tricks and your ace of hearts. This is a general principle of the defence against a cross-ruff: each trump lead saves a trick.

West didn't know that a trump lead was desirable from his point of view. If you had bid the hearts, West might have hit upon the correct opening lead. Part of the art of bidding is to tell the opponents nothing more than necessary. In this case, once your partner had raised spades, you wanted to be in exactly four spades, so there was no need to bid your hearts.

TRUMPS AS ENTRIES

A card that will win a trick is an entry. Sometimes the card is far more valuable as an entry than as a trick-winner. This is true of trumps, as it is of other suits.

37.

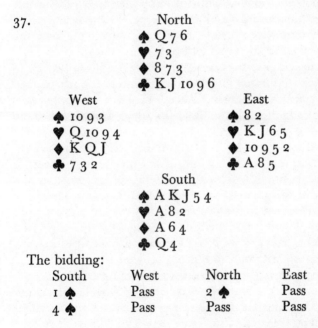

North
♠ Q 7 6
♥ 7 3
♦ 8 7 3
♣ K J 10 9 6

West
♠ 10 9 3
♥ Q 10 9 4
♦ K Q J
♣ 7 3 2

East
♠ 8 2
♥ K J 6 5
♦ 10 9 5 2
♣ A 8 5

South
♠ A K J 5 4
♥ A 8 2
♦ A 6 4
♣ Q 4

The bidding:

South	West	North	East
1 ♠	Pass	2 ♠	Pass
4 ♠	Pass	Pass	Pass

West leads the king of diamonds, and you count your losers: none in trumps, one or two in hearts, two in diamonds, and one in club. You must reduce this loss, since you cannot afford to give up four or five tricks.

Is there a long suit that may furnish discards? Yes; the clubs may do the trick.

You play a low diamond from the dummy, East plays low, and you win with the ace of diamonds. Suppose you next draw three rounds of trumps, exhausting the trumps held by the opponents. Finally, with an air of triumph, you lead the queen of clubs.

'The opponents can take the ace of clubs,' you say to yourself, 'and they can also take two diamonds, but then I shall be able to regain control.' You plan to lead your low club to the dummy and discard your losing hearts.

But something terrible happens! When you lead the queen of clubs the opponents refuse to take the ace! They take the *next* club trick, and now there is no way for you to get back to dummy for all those splendid club tricks.

Do you recognize what has taken place? The opponents have made use of the hold-up play. Declarer has no monopoly on this play.

What can you do to prevent this? You must save an *entry* to the clubs. The only side entry is the queen of spades. You can't draw three rounds of trumps and *then* still have the queen of spades as an entry to the clubs.

The solution to the problem is to draw only *two* rounds of trumps—with the ace and the king—before starting on the clubs. You are well aware that you haven't drawn the last trump, but you can't afford to draw it just yet.

After drawing just two rounds of trumps, you lead the queen of clubs. Nobody takes it, and you lead another club. This time the opponents take the ace and take their two diamond tricks also. Then they lead a heart. You take the ace of hearts and *now* lead a third round of trumps to dummy's queen. This draws West's last trump and *also* gets you into the dummy to cash your good clubs. You can discard your losing hearts on the clubs, and all is well.

PLAY AT A TRUMP CONTRACT

Why didn't you try to ruff a heart in the dummy? You would first have to give up a heart trick in the process. That would allow the enemy to take one heart, two diamonds, and a club—too many tricks.

The Hold-up at a Suit Contract

38.

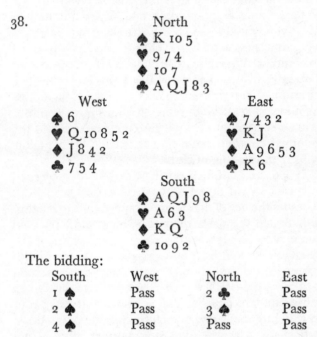

North
♠ K 10 5
♥ 9 7 4
♦ 10 7
♣ A Q J 8 3

West
♠ 6
♥ Q 10 8 5 2
♦ J 8 4 2
♣ 7 5 4

East
♠ 7 4 3 2
♥ K J
♦ A 9 6 5 3
♣ K 6

South
♠ A Q J 9 8
♥ A 6 3
♦ K Q
♣ 10 9 2

The bidding:

South	West	North	East
1 ♠	Pass	2 ♣	Pass
2 ♠	Pass	3 ♠	Pass
4 ♠	Pass	Pass	Pass

West opens the five of hearts, and you count your losers: none in trumps, two in hearts, one in diamonds, and perhaps one in clubs. If the club finesse succeeds, you will have no trouble, for you will then lose only the two hearts and a diamond. You must provide, if you can, for the loss of the club finesse.

Your best chance is to hold-up the ace of hearts in the hope that you can cut the communications between the two opponents. Your aim is to restrict the loss to only one heart trick.

Having made your plan, you play a low heart from the dummy. East puts up the king, and you play *low*. East continues with the knave of hearts, and this time you win the trick. There would be no point in holding up any longer, since then you would lose two heart tricks immediately.

Having won the second round of hearts you next proceed to draw trumps. West discards a low heart on the second round of trumps, so you know that East holds four of the five missing trumps. You proceed to draw all four of them, discarding a low heart from dummy on your fourth trump.

You are now ready to try the club finesse. You lead the ten of clubs from your hand and let it ride for a finesse. East wins with the king of clubs.

This is a disappointment. If the finesse had succeeded your contract would be safe.

East cashes the ace of diamonds. You are glad to see this. If *West* had held the ace of diamonds, he would have used it as an entry to his high heart.

Now East leads another diamond—thanks to your hold-up, he is unable to lead another heart. You win the second round of diamonds with the king and can now safely run the clubs to discard your last losing heart. You make your contract, losing one heart, one club, and one diamond.

The hold-up is less useful at suit contracts than at no-trumps. One reason is that the long suit is not so great a threat when you have a trump suit to furnish stoppers. Another reason is that it's sometimes dangerous to hold up an ace at a suit contract; one of the opponents may have a singleton, and your ace may be ruffed away if you fail to take it the first time.

Nevertheless the hold-up play should not be completely disregarded when you are declarer at a suit contract. It is not strictly a no-trump play.

AVOIDANCE AT A SUIT CONTRACT

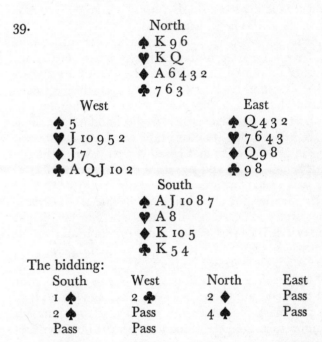

39.
        North
        ♠ K 9 6
        ♥ K Q
        ♦ A 6 4 3 2
        ♣ 7 6 3

West
♠ 5
♥ J 10 9 5 2
♦ J 7
♣ A Q J 10 2

East
♠ Q 4 3 2
♥ 7 6 4 3
♦ Q 9 8
♣ 9 8

        South
        ♠ A J 10 8 7
        ♥ A 8
        ♦ K 10 5
        ♣ K 5 4

The bidding:

South	West	North	East
1 ♠	2 ♣	2 ♦	Pass
2 ♠	Pass	4 ♠	Pass
Pass	Pass		

West opens the knave of hearts, and you count your losers: perhaps one in spades (the queen is out against you), none in hearts, one in diamonds, and perhaps three in clubs. Far too many. You must look for a way to reduce the loss.

What can you do about the possible trump loser? You

have a two-way finesse in spades. (This type of play was explained in Hand No. 23.) If you can guess which opponent has the queen of spades you can finesse through him and avoid the loss of a spade trick.

Even if you can pick up the queen of spades, you may still lose a diamond and three clubs. Your best chance to prevent that loss is to establish dummy's diamonds so that you can discard some of your losers.

In order to establish the diamonds, you will almost surely have to give up a diamond trick to one of the opponents. That opponent had better be *West*, since if East wins the diamond trick he will lead a club through your king, and you will lose three club tricks immediately.

In short, we have here in a single hand played at a trump suit the same situations that you have met at no-trumps in Hand No. 23 and Hand No. 24. One of the opponents is dangerous, and you must develop your tricks in such a way as to shut him out.

Having made your plan, you play the queen of hearts at the first trick and overtake with the ace in your own hand. You may need a heart entry to the dummy later on, so you must win the first trick in your own hand.

Next you start to draw trumps, and there is now a problem when it comes to choosing which way to finesse. Your idea is to finesse the spades in such a way as to lose to *West* if lose you must. Therefore you lead a spade to dummy's king and return the nine of spades from the dummy. East plays low, and you let the nine of spades ride for a finesse.

As it happens, your finesse works. West discards the queen of clubs on dummy's nine of spades. (This high card is a signal asking East to lead clubs.) Now you know that East started with four trumps and that he still has the queen and one small trump.

The lead is still in the dummy because you led the *nine* of spades. (If you had led the *six* of spades, you'd have been obliged to play a higher spade from your hand, and you'd be in the wrong hand at this point.) You are in position to lead another trump from the dummy to repeat the finesse. East plays low, and you win with the knave in your own hand. You can now lead out the ace of spades, catching East's queen. (Dummy discards a low club.)

You have completed the first part of your plan, but you must now develop the diamonds without losing a trick to East. The correct method is to lead a heart to dummy's king and return a small diamond towards your hand. East plays low, and you play the ten in the hope of ducking the trick into the West hand. West wins with the knave of diamonds.

West leads the ten of hearts. Once more you discard a club from the dummy, since you want to keep all of the diamonds, and you ruff with the last trump in your hand. Now you lead the king of diamonds and your low diamond to dummy's ace. All of the outstanding diamonds drop, and you are in position to cash both of dummy's long diamonds. This permits you to discard two clubs, so that you lose *only one* club trick and one diamond in all.

Do you see why it was necessary to begin the development of the diamonds by entering dummy with the king of hearts and then returning a low diamond? The only other way of starting the diamonds is to lead a low diamond to the ace and then return a diamond in order to duck the trick to West's knave. This leaves you with the king of diamonds in your hand and three small diamonds in the dummy. West returns a heart, thus removing dummy's last entry to the diamonds while you still have the king of diamonds in your hand to *block* the suit.

As you can see, it is sometimes necessary to look ahead

in the play to make sure that you can be in the right hand at the right time.

GETTING A QUICK DISCARD

In many hands you can afford to draw trumps either partially or completely before you have to develop your side tricks or take your discards. In some cases, however, you must take your discards at the first possible opportunity since, otherwise, you won't get them at all. In such a case you may not be able to afford even one round of trumps until you have discarded a loser or two.

40.

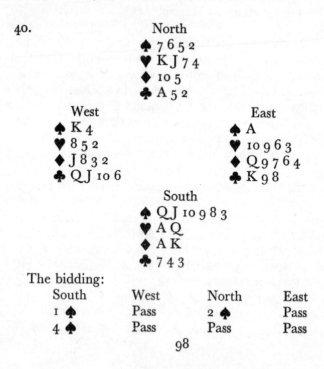

North
♠ 7 6 5 2
♥ K J 7 4
♦ 10 5
♣ A 5 2

West
♠ K 4
♥ 8 5 2
♦ J 8 3 2
♣ Q J 10 6

East
♠ A
♥ 10 9 6 3
♦ Q 9 7 6 4
♣ K 9 8

South
♠ Q J 10 9 8 3
♥ A Q
♦ A K
♣ 7 4 3

The bidding:

South	West	North	East
1 ♠	Pass	2 ♠	Pass
4 ♠	Pass	Pass	Pass

West opens the queen of clubs, and you count your losers: two in spades, and two in clubs. That's one more than you can afford.

It doesn't help you to hold up the ace of clubs. If you take the ace of clubs on the first or second round of the suit, and then lead trumps, the enemy will take two trumps and two clubs.

You must take the ace of clubs (preferably at the first trick), lead a heart to the ace and return the queen of hearts. You can't afford to let the queen of hearts win the trick, for then you'd have no way of getting to dummy's king and knave. You must overtake your own queen of hearts with dummy's king! This enables you to lead the knave of hearts and discard one of your clubs. The contract is now safe since you have only one club loser.

It is still necessary to draw trumps, and you have it in your power to be very tricky. Lead a diamond from dummy to your own hand and then lead the queen of spades. If West is panicky, he will play the king of spades—and his partner will have to win the trick with the blank ace! If West thinks about it he will realize that you cannot have the ace of spades, and he will therefore play his low spade instead of the ace—but it never hurts to give your opponents a chance to do something foolish.

A Ruffer as an Entry

When you are going to ruff a loser with one of dummy's otherwise worthless trumps, plan to do the ruffing when it will do you the most good. Don't be in too much of a hurry.

41.

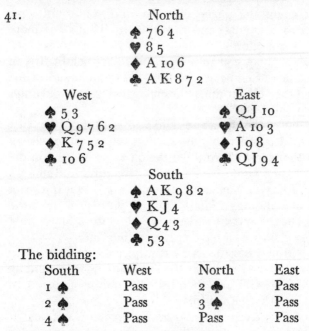

North
- ♠ 7 6 4
- ♥ 8 5
- ♦ A 10 6
- ♣ A K 8 7 2

West
- ♠ 5 3
- ♥ Q 9 7 6 2
- ♦ K 7 5 2
- ♣ 10 6

East
- ♠ Q J 10
- ♥ A 10 3
- ♦ J 9 8
- ♣ Q J 9 4

South
- ♠ A K 9 8 2
- ♥ K J 4
- ♦ Q 4 3
- ♣ 5 3

The bidding:

South	West	North	East
1 ♠	Pass	2 ♣	Pass
2 ♠	Pass	3 ♠	Pass
4 ♠	Pass	Pass	Pass

West leads the six of hearts, and you count your losers: one in hearts (the lead assures your king of a trick, and you plan to ruff one heart in dummy), one in trumps, and one or two in diamonds. The contract is in danger if the diamonds are unfavourably located.

Instead of depending only on good luck in diamonds, you should try to establish dummy's long clubs. One diamond discard is all you need.

Let's see how it works out. You play a low heart from the dummy, and East wins with the ace. East returns the queen of spades, and you win with the ace. (East can see that you will eventually want to ruff a heart, and he is trying to remove the trumps from dummy.)

You can next afford to draw a second round of trumps with the king of spades. This leaves one trump in dummy to ruff your losing heart—but there is no hurry about that. The ruffer will not run away.

Begin to establish the clubs first. Your ruffing trick will be an entry that will help you establish the clubs—if you use it at the right time.

After drawing the two rounds of trumps you cash dummy's top clubs. Then you ruff a club in your own hand. You are not worried about an over-ruff, because that will use up the last trump held by the defenders, and dummy's ruffing trick will still be safe.

As it happens, West discards a heart on the third round of clubs. Now you cash the king of hearts and ruff the knave of hearts with dummy's remaining trump. This is the right time to get to dummy, for now you can lead a fourth round of clubs, ruffing once more in your own hand. This uses up East's last club, and dummy's fifth club is now good.

Should you now lead a trump? No. Somebody has the queen of trumps, but you can afford to ignore it. Just lead a diamond to dummy's ace and lead the last club. You can discard a low diamond, not caring whether or not the queen of spades is used to ruff this trick. If not, you will have ten tricks safely tucked away. If the trick is ruffed, you will make your own last trump for your tenth trick.

Try playing this hand if you ruff a heart *before* beginning on the clubs. You won't be able to get to dummy often enough to establish and cash the fifth club.

COUNTING THE UNSEEN HANDS

If you enjoy detective stories you will get some of the

same thrill out of most bridge hands. You get your evidence from the bidding and play of the enemy, and you use this evidence to reconstruct the exact hand held by each opponent . . . or as nearly exact as possible.

42.

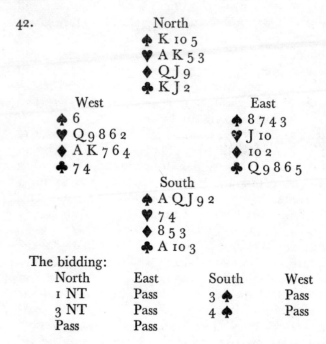

North
♠ K 10 5
♥ A K 5 3
♦ Q J 9
♣ K J 2

West
♠ 6
♥ Q 9 8 6 2
♦ A K 7 6 4
♣ 7 4

East
♠ 8 7 4 3
♥ J 10
♦ 10 2
♣ Q 9 8 6 5

South
♠ A Q J 9 2
♥ 7 4
♦ 8 5 3
♣ A 10 3

The bidding:

North	East	South	West
1 NT	Pass	3 ♠	Pass
3 NT	Pass	4 ♠	Pass
Pass	Pass		

West opens the king of diamonds, and you count your losers: two in diamonds, and one in clubs. Apparently all is well.

You play a low diamond from the dummy, and East plays the *ten*. West next leads the ace of diamonds, and East follows suit with the *deuce*. This high-low asks West to lead the suit again.

West leads a third diamond, and East ruffs. This stroke of

bad luck forces you to reconsider. You have already lost three tricks, and you therefore cannot afford to lose a club trick.

East returns the knave of hearts, and you win in dummy with the king. Your next step is to draw trumps, and you discover that three rounds of trumps are necessary. (Don't forget that East has already used a trump to ruff.) West discards two low diamonds on the second and third rounds of trumps.

You now lead a heart to the ace and return a low heart, ruffing in your own hand. East discards a low club on the third round of hearts.

It is time to assemble the evidence. East began the hand with exactly two diamonds, since he ruffed the third round. He had exactly two hearts, since he discarded on the third round of hearts. East also had four trumps. That accounts for eight of East's thirteen cards. The other five cards must be clubs.

That is as far as we can go with our evidence. We know that East was dealt five of the missing seven clubs; and that West was dealt only two clubs.

Which of them has the queen of clubs? You cannot be sure, but the odds are 5 to 2 that *East* has it. You are not absolutely sure, but even a high degree of probability is better than a sheer guess.

Since you have decided to play East for the queen of clubs, you lead the three of clubs to dummy's king and return a club towards your own hand. East plays low, and you finesse the ten. The finesse succeeds, and you are sure of making your contract.

Note that you always count the cards that an opponent held *originally*—not what he holds later on. It helps to reconstruct an opponent's full hand of thirteen cards because that gives you the chance to check your guesses (if any) by the way your opponent bid and played.

REVERSING THE DUMMY

You usually expect to ruff your losing cards in the dummy and to draw trumps with the trumps in your own hand. Sometimes in order to make your contract you must plan to ruff dummy's losing cards in your own hand and to draw trumps with the dummy's trumps. This topsy-turvy way of playing a hand is called 'reversing the dummy'. You should consider the advisability of following such a plan whenever you are very short of some suit in your own hand.

43.

North
♠ Q J 9
♥ A 7 4 3
♦ Q 10 4
♣ 5 4 2

West
♠ 4 3 2
♥ K Q J 9
♦ 8 5
♣ A Q J 9

East
♠ 6 5
♥ 10 8 6 2
♦ 9 7 6 3 2
♣ K 10

South
♠ A K 10 8 7
♥ 5
♦ A K J
♣ 8 7 6 3

The bidding:

South	West	North	East
1 ♠	Pass	2 ♠	Pass
3 ♣	Pass	4 ♠	Pass
Pass	Pass		

West opens the king of hearts, and you count your losers: three or four in clubs. What can you do to make sure that you lose only three tricks and not four?

One plan is to take the first trick and lead a club at once. You will lead clubs at every opportunity, hoping to ruff your fourth club in dummy if either opponent still has a club. (If each opponent has three clubs, your last club will be good even if you don't ruff it.)

This seems like a good plan, and nobody could blame you for adopting it. There are some flaws in it, however, and we may want to look for a different plan after we have considered the dangers of this one.

If the opponents are on their toes, they will lead trumps at every opportunity. By the time you have led three clubs, they will have led three trumps. That will leave dummy without a trump for your fourth club. Of course, the opponents may not be on their toes and may therefore fail to lead trumps promptly; or the player who wins the third round of clubs may then be out of trumps; or the clubs may break 3-3. Hence your plan isn't doomed to failure; it isn't, however, sure-fire.

There is a second danger. One of the opponents may be short in diamonds. If you lead clubs without drawing trumps, the opponents may lead diamonds back at you, and one of them may get a ruffing trick to set the contract.

Both of these dangers (trump returns or diamond returns) are fairly remote. They are pointed out largely so that you can see what a good bridge player thinks about.

A safer plan is to reverse the dummy by ruffing hearts in the South hand. Since you plan to ruff often in your own hand, you count *winners* instead of losers. You will ruff all three of dummy's low hearts in your hand, and you will draw three rounds of trumps from the dummy—for a total of six trump tricks. You will also make the ace of hearts and your three top diamonds. The total is ten tricks, just enough for your contract.

Let's put it into operation to see how it works. You win the first heart with dummy's ace and return a heart to ruff with the seven of spades. You lead the eight of spades to dummy's nine and return a second low heart to ruff—with the king of trumps!

This leaves the ten of spades in your hand, and you lead it to dummy's knave. The idea of ruffing *high* is just to make sure that you can conveniently get back to dummy with a trump. Now you can lead dummy's last low heart and ruff it with your last trump, the ace.

You return to dummy by leading the knave of diamonds and overtaking with dummy's queen. This enables you to lead dummy's queen of trumps to draw the last trump held by the enemy. You are already out of trumps, so you discard one of your four low clubs! (You never thought you'd get rid of a club *that* way, did you?)

And now you can safely cash your remaining top diamonds to assure the contract.

This is a better plan than the first one, but it takes a bit of imagination to see it and a bit of thinking to work it out so that you can get to the right hand at the right time. At this stage of your bridge career, nobody will blame you if you miss this kind of play—provided that you adopt some reasonable plan like the project of ruffing out the fourth club. The only real crime is to play the hand without any plan at all.

The Bath Coup

Our next play is named after the West Country resort, Bath, where in the heyday of whist, it was first invented. The idea, as shown in the following hand, is to refuse the first heart trick when West leads the king and you, South, hold ace-knave small.

If you play the low heart quickly enough and with every appearance of innocence, West may be foolish enough to lead a second heart. Whether he leads the queen or a low heart, this will enable you to win two heart tricks.

44.

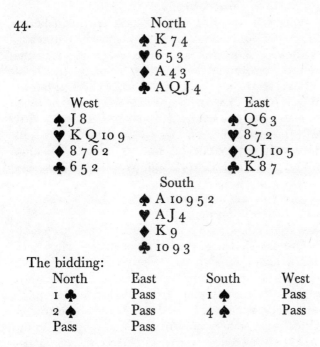

North
♠ K 7 4
♥ 6 5 3
♦ A 4 3
♣ A Q J 4

West
♠ J 8
♥ K Q 10 9
♦ 8 7 6 2
♣ 6 5 2

East
♠ Q 6 3
♥ 8 7 2
♦ Q J 10 5
♣ K 8 7

South
♠ A 10 9 5 2
♥ A J 4
♦ K 9
♣ 10 9 3

The bidding:

North	East	South	West
1 ♣	Pass	1 ♠	Pass
2 ♠	Pass	4 ♠	Pass
Pass	Pass		

Even if West is clever enough to *shift* (lead another suit), you will still gain by your use of the Bath Coup. This shift will leave the ace of hearts in your hand. This is important, because you fear the loss of a spade and a club, so you cannot afford to lose more than one heart trick.

West wins the first heart with his king and then leads a

diamond. You win with the king of diamonds, draw two rounds of trumps with the king and then the ace, after which you lead the ten of clubs for a finesse. You don't draw a third trump; the opponent who has the queen of spades is at liberty to take a trick with it whenever he likes. Note that you win the second trump in your own hand in order to start the clubs correctly.

East wins with the king of clubs and returns a heart. You put up the ace of hearts and go back to the clubs, still leaving the queen of trumps at large. When you lead the fourth club from dummy, you can discard the knave of hearts. East can ruff this trick or not, as he chooses, but he can get only one trick with his queen of spades in any case.

You would lose the contract if you took the very first trick with the ace of hearts. You would draw two rounds of trumps and then try the club finesse, losing to the king. East would then lead a heart, and West would take *two* heart tricks. And down you would go.

Let's stay with this hand for a moment, while we examine a few other interesting points. Why did you refrain from leading a third round of trumps? It would have been fatal to give East the lead with the queen of spades. He would have led a heart, making you take your ace; and East would have regained the lead with the king of clubs to lead another heart before you could get a discard on the clubs.

What would happen if East had only two clubs instead of three clubs? East would then ruff the third round of clubs, while you were still following suit and before you could discard a heart. This would enable East to lead hearts for the third time, defeating the contract. This would be too bad for you, of course, but you would have the consolation of knowing that you had done your best.

This also raises an interesting defensive pointer. If East does hold only two clubs, he must ruff immediately when the third club is led. If he makes the mistake of discarding on the assumption that his queen of spades will be just as good later, South will win the third club in dummy and lead a fourth club to discard the knave of hearts. You are going to learn more about defensive play later in this book, but it does no harm to learn a little at this moment. When declarer is trying to get fast discards, defenders should step in promptly with a trump to prevent the discard.

The heart situation is very instructive. It would be much the same if the hearts were as follows:

45.
　　　　　　　　　North
　　　　　　　　　♥ A 5 3
West　　　　　　　　　　　　　East
♥ K Q 10 9　　　　　　　　　♥ 8 7 2
　　　　　　　　　South
　　　　　　　　　♥ J 6 4

West leads the king of hearts, and South must play low from the dummy. If West continues by leading the queen of hearts, dummy wins with the ace, and South's knave is then high. If West continues by leading the ten or nine of hearts, South plays low from the dummy and wins with the knave at once. Either way, a heart continuation gives declarer two heart tricks. If West is clever enough to shift to a different suit, South gains time, as in Hand No. 44, to get a discard.

This situation is very different:

46.
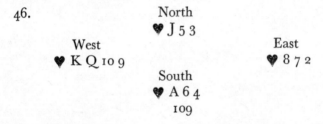

　　　　　　　　　North
　　　　　　　　　♥ J 5 3
West　　　　　　　　　　　　　East
♥ K Q 10 9　　　　　　　　　♥ 8 7 2
　　　　　　　　　South
　　　　　　　　　♥ A 6 4

If West leads the king of hearts, South must take the ace at once. Then or later, South can lead a low heart towards dummy's knave to make sure of winning a trick with it. There is no need to employ a hold-up or the Bath Coup, for South can develop a second heart trick by sheer force.

The same thing is true if declarer holds the ten of hearts, either in his own hand or in the dummy, in addition to the ace and knave. He can capture the king with his ace, return the knave to force out the queen, and thus establish the ten of hearts to win the third round of the suit.

SAFETY AND PERCENTAGE PLAYS

By this time you should be used to the idea that you begin a suit by winning the first trick in the *short* hand. You may make an exception if you have an urgent need to win a trick in a particular hand at a particular time. There are exceptions to practically all of the rules for good play.

When the 'short' hand is only relatively short—say it has three or more cards—you may decide to win the first trick in the *long* hand. There is still time to play the suit in such a manner as to keep out of your own way.

47.

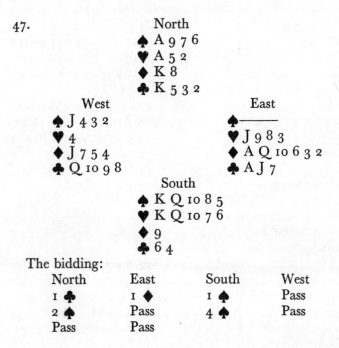

North
♠ A 9 7 6
♥ A 5 2
♦ K 8
♣ K 5 3 2

West
♠ J 4 3 2
♥ 4
♦ J 7 5 4
♣ Q 10 9 8

East
♠ ——
♥ J 9 8 3
♦ A Q 10 6 3 2
♣ A J 7

South
♠ K Q 10 8 5
♥ K Q 10 7 6
♦ 9
♣ 6 4

The bidding:

North	East	South	West
1 ♣	1 ♦	1 ♠	Pass
2 ♠	Pass	4 ♠	Pass
Pass	Pass		

West opens the four of diamonds, and you count your losers: one in diamonds, and one or two in clubs . . . provided that you can play both spades and hearts without loss. And that is your whole problem in this hand—to play the major suits without loss.

Let's see how it works out. You put up the king of diamonds from the dummy at the first trick—not with much hope but mostly because it costs nothing to try. But East wins with the ace, just as you expected. East returns the queen of diamonds, and you ruff with the five of spades.

Your first task is to draw trumps. Dummy is the original short trump hand, but you don't win the first trump trick in dummy. You begin the trumps by leading the king from your hand.

Your reason is that you want to find out whether or not one of the opponents has all four of the missing trumps. And you want to find out while it is still possible to finesse for the knave of spades *in either direction*.

As it happens, East discards a diamond on the first round of trumps. This tells you that West has all four of the missing trumps. You are in position to lead a small trump in order to finesse dummy's nine. You would not be able to do so if you had begun the spades by winning with dummy's ace.

Suppose *West* had discarded on the first round of trumps. You would then know that *East* had all of the trumps. You would lead a second trump to the ace and return a trump to finesse your ten.

The situation would be the same if you exchanged the ace and king of spades or the ace and queen of spades. You win the first trick in the hand that has *two* high cards, thus saving one high card in each hand. This still gives you a two-way finesse for the second trick by the time you know which way you want to finesse.

When you have drawn all four rounds of trumps, you must now play the hearts in such a way as to lose no tricks. The correct method is to win the second trick in the short hand.

By the time you have played two rounds of the suit you will know whether or not you need a finesse on the third round of hearts. You won't know any earlier, and you don't want to guess.

Naturally, you can't begin the hearts by taking the *second* trick. But you know that you want to win the second heart with dummy's ace, so you win the first heart with the king in your own hand. After that, you lead a low heart to dummy's ace. This time *West* discards a diamond, so you know that East has the rest of the hearts. You are in the dummy, having won the trick with the ace. This puts you in position to lead a low heart and finesse the ten in order to pick up East's knave without loss.

The rest of the hand is, of course, very easy. You win five spade tricks and five heart tricks. The opponents take one diamond and two clubs.

Incidentally, you were very lucky to be playing the hand at four spades. West should raise diamonds instead of passing, and then East would not sell out so tamely. If East were allowed to play the hand at diamonds he would make twelve tricks! You must take full advantage of the enemy's cowardice by playing the cards properly at four spades.

There are other safety plays besides the two described in the comment on Hand No. 47. There is no need to burden your memory with them at this stage of your bridge career. By the time you are ready for them you may be able to work them out for yourself—or perhaps you will look for them in the book that I plan to write on *advanced* bidding and play.

FOUR

Defending Against No-trump Contracts

Defending against a no-trump contract is largely a matter of establishing and cashing your tricks before declarer manages to establish and cash his. You and your partner will seldom have enough strength to set the contract with high cards alone, so you must try to bring in some long suit.

Your best chance to bring in a long suit lies in opening a good suit to begin with and then in hammering away at that suit as often as possible. If you switch aimlessly from one suit to another, you will help declarer.

If you are the opening leader, how do you pick a good suit? You look for a suit in which you or your partner has length (four cards or more) and in which declarer has only one or two stoppers at most.

If your partner has bid a suit, that usually solves your problem. Lead his suit, for your partner will surely have length and strength, together with a side entry or two. Don't be discouraged by the fact that the opponents have bid no-trumps after hearing your partner bid his suit. Declarer surely has a stopper or two in your partner's suit, but that suit is usually your best bet anyway.

When your partner has not bid, it is up to you to find the

best partnership suit on your own. This is usually the best suit in your own hand, but sometimes you must try to find your partner's best suit because of the weakness of your own hand.

When you are trying to guess at the best partnership suit avoid leading a suit that has been bid by the opponents. The enemy will usually have length and strength in the suits that they have bid; and your object is to find a suit in which they do *not*.

Occasionally, you may lead through dummy's bid suit if you have two or three worthless cards in that suit. You hope that the dummy's holding is not too strong and that your partner will be in position to win any finesse that may be tried. You do *not* lead a suit that has been bid by *declarer*, however, since that is sure to give declarer a free finesse.

LEADING YOUR PARTNER'S BID SUIT

The correct opening lead in your partner's suit depends partly on the number of cards you have in the suit and partly on the high cards you may have in the suit.

Singleton: No choice. You have only one card, and you lead it. (If you have a really good suit of your own, you might try that suit instead.)

Doubleton: Lead the *higher* of your two cards.

Tripleton: With three small cards, lead your highest card. With two or more 'touching' (consecutive) honours, lead the highest of the honours. Otherwise, lead the lowest card.

Four: With two or more touching honours, lead the highest of the honours. Otherwise, lead the lowest card.

In these examples, the card to lead is underlined:

A 3	K 5	J 4	8 2	
10 7 3	9 8 4	8 6 2		
K Q 3	Q J 2	J 10 4		
A 5 4	K 6 2	Q 7 3	J 5 2	Q 10 5
J 10 4 2	K Q 3 2	Q J 5 2		
A 7 6 2	K 6 5 3	Q 6 3 2	J 5 3 2	9 6 3 2

Use the same principles for leading when you are trying to *guess* at your partner's best suit.

LEADING YOUR OWN BEST SUIT

When your best suit is headed by *three* or more honours, you lead one of the honours. Otherwise, you lead the fourth-highest card, counting down from the top.

K-Q-J-8-3. Lead the king, the top card of three honours in sequence.

K-Q-10-8-3. Lead the king, treating this holding as though it were three honours in unbroken sequence.

K-Q-7-6-3. Lead the six, the fourth-highest card.

Q-J-10-8-3. Lead the queen, top of three touching honours.

Q-J-9-6-3. Lead the queen, treating this holding as though it were three honours in unbroken sequence.

Q-J-7-5-3-2. Lead the five, fourth-highest card.

A-Q-J-7-4. Lead the queen, top of an *inside* sequence.

K-J-10-7-4. Lead the jack, top of an inside sequence.

A-J-10-7-4. Lead the jack, top of an inside sequence.

K-10-9-7-4. Lead the ten, top of an inside sequence.

Q-10-9-6-3-2. Lead the ten, top of an inside sequence.

A-10-9-7-5. Lead the ten, top of an inside sequence.

J-10-9-6-4. Lead the jack, top of a sequence.

J-10-8-6-4. Lead the jack, treating it as in the last case.
J-10-6-5-4-2. Lead the five, fourth-highest card.
A-Q-9-5-3-2. Lead the five, fourth-highest card.
K-J-8-7-5-3. Lead the seven, fourth-highest card.
K-Q-8-7-4-2. Lead the seven, fourth-highest card.
A-J-9-8-5-3. Lead the eight, fourth-highest card.
Q-6-5-4-2. Lead the four, fourth-highest card.
J-9-8-7-3-2. Lead the seven, fourth-highest card.
K-9-8-5-4. Lead the five, fourth-highest card.
A-9-7-4-3-2. Lead the four, fourth-highest card.

We are now ready to see some examples of defensive play
in operation.

STARTING THE RIGHT SUIT

48.

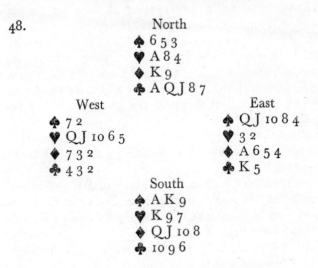

North
♠ 6 5 3
♥ A 8 4
♦ K 9
♣ A Q J 8 7

West
♠ 7 2
♥ Q J 10 6 5
♦ 7 3 2
♣ 4 3 2

East
♠ Q J 10 8 4
♥ 3 2
♦ A 6 5 4
♣ K 5

South
♠ A K 9
♥ K 9 7
♦ Q J 10 8
♣ 10 9 6

117

DEFENDING AGAINST NO-TRUMP CONTRACTS

The bidding:

North	East	South	West
1 ♣	1 ♠	2 NT	Pass
3 NT	Pass	Pass	Pass

West must lead spades, his partner's bid suit. Since he has a doubleton he leads the higher card, the seven of spades.

Dummy plays low, and East plays the ten of spades. If East were *leading* spades, he would lead the queen, the *top* card of his sequence. Since East is trying to win the trick (or to force out a higher card), he plays the *lowest* card of the sequence.

You may hear somebody quote the rule 'Third hand *high*'. This means that the third player to play to a trick should play high enough to win the trick or to force out a higher card from the fourth player. However, third hand should play the lowest card that will do the job when he has cards of equal value. In this case, the queen, knave, and ten are of equal value, and East must play the ten.

South wins with the king of spades and leads the ten of clubs for a finesse. East wins with the king of clubs and returns the queen of spades.

East must keep plugging away at the spades. Note that East *leads* the *top* card of his sequence. South wins with the ace of spades.

South now goes back to the clubs, running the rest of dummy's long suit. On the third round of clubs East discards the six of diamonds. On the fourth club, East discards the four of diamonds. This high-low is a signal to tell West (who can see only his own hand and the dummy) that East has strength in diamonds.

Why does East want to signal his strength? If West happens to win a trick, the signal will tell him to lead a diamond. This isn't very likely, and West would probably lead a diamond anyway. Far more important is the fact that West may have trouble finding safe discards on the dummy's long clubs; the signal tells him that he can safely discard diamonds, since East can take care of that suit.

Dummy continues with the fifth round of clubs, and East discards a third low diamond. West discards one low diamond and one low heart (or two low diamonds).

South cannot make nine tricks without going after a diamond trick. Now, the moment declarer leads a diamond, East will take the ace of diamonds, cash the knave of spades and then take his two low spades (which will be established by then). East will set the contract with one club, one diamond, and three spades.

Note that South would have made his contract if the defenders had failed to lead spades at every opportunity. For example, suppose that West opens the queen of hearts instead of a spade. South wins and loses a club finesse to East. It does East no good to lead another heart, since West will never be able to regain the lead to cash his established hearts (which is why he shouldn't lead the suit to begin with). It is also too late for East to switch to spades. South can win with the king of spades, knock out the ace of diamonds, regain the lead with the ace of spades, and then take eleven tricks.

Leading the Right Card in Partner's Suit

49.

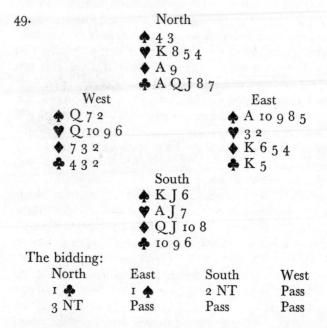

North
♠ 4 3
♥ K 8 5 4
♦ A 9
♣ A Q J 8 7

West
♠ Q 7 2
♥ Q 10 9 6
♦ 7 3 2
♣ 4 3 2

East
♠ A 10 9 8 5
♥ 3 2
♦ K 6 5 4
♣ K 5

South
♠ K J 6
♥ A J 7
♦ Q J 10 8
♣ 10 9 6

The bidding:

North	East	South	West
1 ♣	1 ♠	2 NT	Pass
3 NT	Pass	Pass	Pass

West must lead spades, his partner's bid suit. Since he has Q-x-x, West must lead the lowest card, the deuce in this case. East puts up the ace of spades, winning the trick, and returns the ten of spades through South's king-knave. South finesses the knave, and West wins with the queen.

South is thus limited to one spade trick, the king. West naturally leads his last spade after winning the second trick with the queen of spades. This knocks out the king of spades, setting up the rest of East's suit.

South must lead the ten of clubs for a finesse, since he will make his contract if he can win five club tricks. The finesse loses, however, to East's king. East gets a club and four spades, defeating the contract.

South would make his contract if West makes the mistake of opening the *queen* of spades instead of the deuce. No matter how East plays, South is bound to make both the king and the knave of spades after West opens the queen. This gives declarer time enough to develop his nine tricks.

For example, suppose that after East takes the first trick with the ace of spades he returns the ten of spades. South wins with the knave of spades and tries the club finesse. East wins with the king of clubs and leads another spade. South wins with the king of spades and runs nine tricks: two spades, four clubs, two hearts, and one diamond.

This hand illustrates the reason for leading a low card when you have A-x-x, K-x-x, Q-x-x, or J-x-x of your partner's suit. The idea is to keep your high card 'behind' declarer. He certainly holds spade stoppers, as he bid no trump over East's spade bid. You keep *your* high spade so that you can capture some lesser honour held by declarer when East leads through him.

To take another example, suppose you have J-x-x of your partner's suit. Your partner has A-K-x-x-x and declarer has Q-10-x-x. If you lead the knave, declarer has two stoppers in the suit. (Leave the cards out and prove this is true.) If you lead low, your partner will win with the king and return a low card through declarer. Declarer will be able to win a trick with his queen, but he will never win a trick with the ten.

LEADING YOUR OWN LONG SUIT

50.

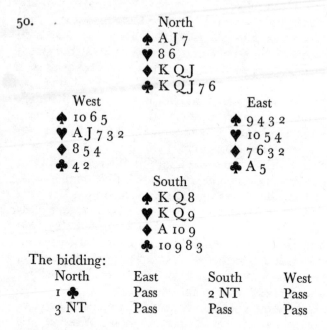

North
- ♠ A J 7
- ♥ 8 6
- ♦ K Q J
- ♣ K Q J 7 6

West
- ♠ 10 6 5
- ♥ A J 7 3 2
- ♦ 8 5 4
- ♣ 4 2

East
- ♠ 9 4 3 2
- ♥ 10 5 4
- ♦ 7 6 3 2
- ♣ A 5

South
- ♠ K Q 8
- ♥ K Q 9
- ♦ A 10 9
- ♣ 10 9 8 3

The bidding:

North	East	South	West
1 ♣	Pass	2 NT	Pass
3 NT	Pass	Pass	Pass

West must choose the opening lead without having received any help from his partner's bidding. The long heart suit is an obvious choice. West leads the three of hearts, the fourth-highest card in the suit.

Perhaps you wonder why you are told to lead the *fourth*-highest card in a case of this kind. If you were just trying to establish your long suit, *any* low card would make a good opening lead—whether it happened to be fourth-highest, fifth-highest, or whatever. But you often need your partner's help in establishing your suit, and you therefore try to give him information to help him choose the best defence. Your partner gets more reliable information if you are consistent about leading fourth-highest than if you sometimes lead one card and sometimes another.

Likewise, consistency is important in the opening lead from a sequence of honours. If you have a suit headed by Q-J-10, you can produce the same effect whether you lead the queen, the knave, or the ten. The only reason for choosing one card consistently rather than another is to give your partner information. When you lead the queen of a suit, your partner will know that you have the knave and either the ten or the nine. He will also know that you do *not* hold the king.

To return to our present hand, dummy plays a low heart and East puts up the ten of hearts. East follows the normal rule of *third hand high*.

South wins the trick with the queen of hearts and leads a club. He needs club tricks to make his contract, and he will be safe if West has the ace of clubs because a heart continuation from the *West* hand will permit South to take a second heart trick with the king.

East wins the first club trick with the ace and returns the *five* of hearts. The general practice is to return the *highest* card in your partner's suit.

South plays the nine of hearts, and West wins with the knave. West knows that the king and four of hearts are missing, and continues with the ace of hearts in the hope that they will both drop. As it happens, they do, and West is able to continue with the seven and then the deuce of hearts. The contract is set since the defenders take one club and four heart tricks.

Note how important it was for the defenders to open the right suit and to keep leading that suit. If West led any other suit to start with, South could safely knock out the ace of clubs. No long suit could be run against him, and he would make four clubs, three spades, three diamonds, and one heart—*eleven* tricks.

Partnership Detective Work

In Hand No. 48 we saw the rule for the play by third hand, but we didn't go into the reasons. They will appear in this hand.

51.

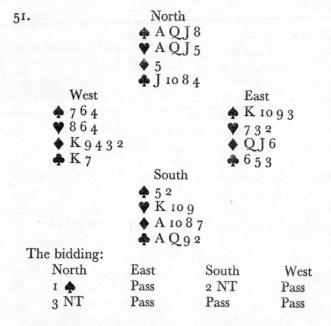

North
♠ A Q J 8
♥ A Q J 5
♦ 5
♣ J 10 8 4

West
♠ 7 6 4
♥ 8 6 4
♦ K 9 4 3 2
♣ K 7

East
♠ K 10 9 3
♥ 7 3 2
♦ Q J 6
♣ 6 5 3

South
♠ 5 2
♥ K 10 9
♦ A 10 8 7
♣ A Q 9 2

The bidding:

North	East	South	West
1 ♠	Pass	2 NT	Pass
3 NT	Pass	Pass	Pass

West leads the three of diamonds, fourth-highest card in his longest suit. Dummy plays the low card, East puts up the knave, and South wins with the ace.

Declarer begins by running his four heart tricks, hoping

that the defenders will discard unwisely. As it happens, however, they have no trouble at all. East discards a low club, and West discards a low spade. South also discards a low spade and must now go on to his main play for the contract.

After running the hearts, declarer leads the knave of clubs from the dummy and lets it ride for a finesse. West wins with the king of clubs and must find the right way to run the rest of the long diamond suit to defeat the contract.

Put yourself in West's place, seeing your own hand and the dummy, but nothing else. Your partner, East, played the knave of diamonds at the first trick, and South won with the ace. Who has the queen of diamonds?

There are only two possibilities. Either South has the queen of diamonds, or East has it. If South had the queen, he would be delighted to win the first trick with it, saving his ace of diamonds for a later trick. But since South actually won the first trick with the *ace* of diamonds, he cannot have the queen. Therefore you know that East must have that queen of diamonds.

Once you have come to this conclusion, it is easy for you to make the correct play. You lead the deuce of diamonds after you win a trick with the king of clubs. East wins with the queen of diamonds and returns his last diamond. This permits you to win a finesse, since you have K-9-4 behind declarer's 10-8. No matter what South does you can win the rest of the diamonds, first taking the two higher cards and then the four. You therefore defeat the contract with one club and four diamonds.

This hand shows why the rule is for third hand to play the lower (or lowest) of touching honours. If East were not trying to give his partner information, he could play either the queen or the knave of diamonds at the first trick, for either card would have the effect of driving out the ace.

The point is, however, that East does want to inform his partner. The play of the knave does permit West to work out who has the queen. But if East played the queen at the first trick there would be no way for West to work out who held the knave. The correct play by third hand doesn't always make the situation clear to both defenders, but it *often* does—and that's better than nothing.

Third Hand 'Not-So-High'

If your partner leads, you will be the third player on that trick. Your normal course is to play your highest card (hence the rule *third hand high*) in order to win the trick or to drive out a higher card from the hand of the fourth player.

As we have seen, this rule is slightly changed when you have one or more cards in sequence with your highest card. You then play the *lowest* card of those 'equals'.

The rule is also changed when you can win a finesse. For example, if your partner leads through dummy's king and you have the ace-queen, you finesse the queen instead of playing *high* with your ace. Here is another example of a finesse by third hand.

52.

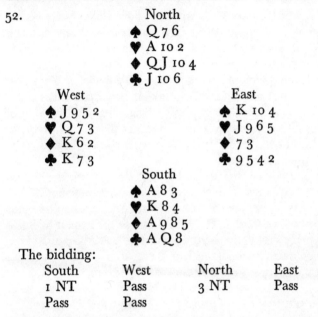

North
♠ Q 7 6
♥ A 10 2
♦ Q J 10 4
♣ J 10 6

West
♠ J 9 5 2
♥ Q 7 3
♦ K 6 2
♣ K 7 3

East
♠ K 10 4
♥ J 9 6 5
♦ 7 3
♣ 9 5 4 2

South
♠ A 8 3
♥ K 8 4
♦ A 9 8 5
♣ A Q 8

The bidding:

South	West	North	East
1 NT	Pass	3 NT	Pass
Pass	Pass		

West opens the deuce of spades, and declarer plays the six of spades from the dummy. If East plays third hand *high*, putting up the king of spades, South will make the contract.

South will capture the king of spades with the ace, and is then assured of two spades, two hearts, a diamond, and a club. To fulfil his contract, South must develop both the diamonds and the clubs and West will get both of his kings. West can manage to establish his spades, but he will get only two spade tricks in addition to his two kings. South makes the remaining nine tricks, and thus makes his contract.

There is a different story to tell if East finesses the ten of spades at the first trick. South wins with the ace of spades and enters dummy with the ace of hearts in order to try the diamond finesse. West takes the king of diamonds and leads the knave of spades in order to make the situation quite clear to his partner.

Now the queen of spades is 'killed'. If declarer plays it at once—as his only chance to make it (this play takes courage, but it is South's best play)—East wins with the king of spades and returns the suit. If dummy plays the low spade instead of the queen, the knave wins the trick, and West leads the suit again.

In either case the defenders get *three* spade tricks and West's two kings. The contract is therefore defeated.

We have just seen that East should finesse when he holds the K-10-4 of spades. He should finesse the nine if he holds K-9-4. He should finesse the eight if he holds K-8-4. In fact, he can hardly lose if he keeps the king to kill dummy's queen, playing some middle-sized spade to the first trick.

In general, you will get the most out of your high cards if you use them to capture (or, at any rate, to cover) the slightly lower cards held by the other side. It seldom pays to play your high cards on the enemy's *low* cards—unless your side has so many high cards that you can well afford to be wasteful.

THE RULE OF ELEVEN

How many spades are higher than the deuce? Twelve, of course. How many are higher than the seven of spades? The answer doesn't come quite so quickly.

You can get a very quick answer if you subtract the number of the card from fourteen. Try it, and see how easy it is.

When the opener leads his fourth-highest card, he naturally has three higher cards of that suit in his hand. If you want to rule out those three higher cards, you can subtract the lead from eleven (instead of from fourteen) to get the number of higher cards in the other three hands—that is, in the hand of the dummy, the leader's partner, and the declarer.

53.

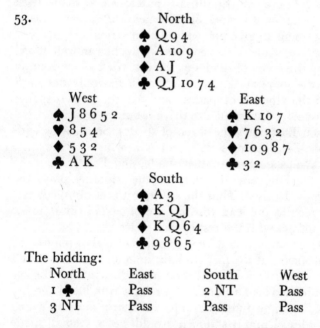

North
♠ Q 9 4
♥ A 10 9
♦ A J
♣ Q J 10 7 4

West
♠ J 8 6 5 2
♥ 8 5 4
♦ 5 3 2
♣ A K

East
♠ K 10 7
♥ 7 6 3 2
♦ 10 9 8 7
♣ 3 2

South
♠ A 3
♥ K Q J
♦ K Q 6 4
♣ 9 8 6 5

The bidding:

North	East	South	West
1 ♣	Pass	2 NT	Pass
3 NT	Pass	Pass	Pass

West leads the five of spades. This is his fourth-best spade. East subtracts the number of the card led from eleven. Five from eleven leaves six. This means that there are six spades higher than the opening lead in the dummy, the East hand, and the South hand, all together.

East sees two spades higher than the five in the dummy —the queen and the nine. He sees three spades higher than the five in his his own hand—the king, the ten, and the seven. That accounts for five cards higher than the five. Therefore there can be only one higher card in the South hand.

It is clear that South must have the ace or the knave of spades, for he wouldn't jump to two no-trumps with the spades 'wide open'. South is sure to get one spade trick whether he holds the ace or the knave; *but* it takes careful management to give him only the one trick!

Using the Rule of Eleven, East knows he can well afford to play the seven of spades at the first trick when dummy plays the four. He knows that South has only one card higher than the five of spades—and that the seven of spades is therefore good enough to drive it out.

When East plays the seven of spades, South wins with the ace. South leads a club, and West wins with the king. Now West can lead another spade, and East must make both the king and the ten, whether dummy plays the queen or the nine. Thus the spade suit is established, and West regains the lead with his ace of clubs in time to set the contract with the rest of the spades.

The situation would be very different if East played the ten of spades at the first trick (as he might do if he didn't know the Rule of Eleven). South would win with the ace of spades and lead a club. West would win and lead another spade, but now dummy's nine would force out East's king of spades. Dummy's queen would be a second spade stopper.

South has no trouble if he can make a second spade trick. He can take three hearts and four diamonds together with the two spades, for a total of nine tricks.

The Rule of Eleven is often used by the declarer as well as by the leader's partner. The declarer subtracts the lead from eleven, notes the number of higher cards in the dummy and in his own hand, and then knows how many higher cards are held by the leader's partner.

A Shift in Time

As we have seen, it usually pays to open a good suit and to stick to that suit. If the opening lead is obviously an unwise choice, however, there may be time to shift to a better suit.

54.

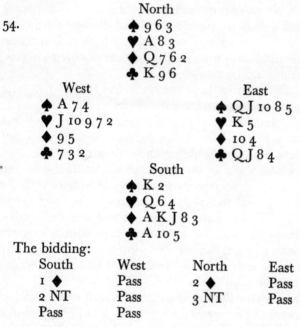

North
♠ 9 6 3
♥ A 8 3
♦ Q 7 6 2
♣ K 9 6

West
♠ A 7 4
♥ J 10 9 7 2
♦ 9 5
♣ 7 3 2

East
♠ Q J 10 8 5
♥ K 5
♦ 10 4
♣ Q J 8 4

South
♠ K 2
♥ Q 6 4
♦ A K J 8 3
♣ A 10 5

The bidding:

South	West	North	East
1 ♦	Pass	2 ♦	Pass
2 NT	Pass	3 NT	Pass
Pass	Pass		

West opens the knave of hearts, the top of a sequence in his best suit. It looks like a reasonable opening lead, but it happens that South has two stoppers in hearts.

South plays a low heart from the dummy at the first trick, and East wins with the king. Now it's East's turn to do a bit of thinking and planning. He knows that South has the queen of hearts, because if West had held the queen together with his knave and his other high hearts, he would have led the queen instead of the knave. (In general the lead of any honour *denies* the next higher honour.)

East therefore knows that South has two sure heart tricks. East suspects that South also has five diamond tricks and one high card in each of the black suits. (South probably wouldn't bid no-trumps with either black suit wide open.) East can see the king of clubs in the dummy and the queen-knave in his own hand. Hence South's high club must be the ace—and South must have nine fast tricks (two hearts, five diamonds, and two clubs).

The only defensive hope is to grab five tricks *before South can gain the lead!* East must shift to the queen of spades in the hope that South has only the king of spades, and that West has the ace. (It might be the other way around, but then there is no way to defeat the contract.)

When East shifts to the queen of spades at the second trick, South hopefully puts up the king. West wins with the ace of spades and returns the seven (his highest remaining card in East's suit). East takes the ten and knave of spades, establishing the eight and the five. East wins five spade tricks and a heart, setting the contract two tricks. Any other return at the second trick would have allowed declarer to take nine fast tricks.

It was easy for East to find the right shift because he *led up to weakness.* You try to make a weak hand play last to a trick in the hope that your partner (who is third hand) will be able to win finesses since he plays after the opponent who is second hand.

For exactly the same reason, you try to lead a suit in

which your partner has strength *behind* an opponent's strength. This is called *leading through strength*.

When the dummy is at your left, you try to lead a suit in which dummy has broken strength. You hope that your partner has the rest of the high cards in that suit. When the dummy is at your right, you usually lead a suit in which dummy has weakness.

Mind you, these are just *general* indications of the best suit to lead. When you have a good definite reason to lead a particular suit, lead it and don't worry about general rules. But if you have no clear course to follow, use the general rule.

LEADING A BID SUIT

55.

North
♠ A Q 10 3
♥ 5 3
♦ A 10 6
♣ K 9 5 3

West
♠ 7 6 5
♥ K J 8 7
♦ J 7 5
♣ J 8 6

East
♠ K J 9 2
♥ 4 2
♦ Q 8 4 2
♣ Q 7 4

South
♠ 8 4
♥ A Q 10 9 6
♦ K 9 3
♣ A 10 2

The bidding:

South	West	North	East
1 ♥	Pass	1 ♠	Pass
1 NT	Pass	3 NT	Pass
Pass	Pass		

DEFENDING AGAINST NO-TRUMP CONTRACTS

West's longest suit has been bid by declarer, so he decides against leading a heart. Nobody could criticize West if he led a low club or a low diamond—the unbid suits. West actually chooses to lead the seven of spades. This kind of lead is called 'the top of nothing'.

South mustn't put up dummy's ace of spades, since that would 'open up' the entire suit. He may play *low* from dummy, or he may try a finesse of the ten or the queen. East plays the lowest card that will win the trick—the nine, if dummy plays low; the knave if dummy plays the ten; the king if dummy plays the queen.

East knows that West's opening lead is not fourth-highest. The Rule of Eleven would show four cards higher than the seven, but East can see *six* spades higher than the seven in his own hand and the dummy. Since the lead therefore cannot be a fourth-highest, East recognizes it as a top-of-nothing lead.

Having won the first spade trick, East must shift to a different suit; it is clearly foolish to return a spade and thus give dummy a free finesse. (This is the most elementary example of shifting away from the suit that is opened.)

East sees that a diamond or a club shift plays *up* to dummy's strength and he prefers to lead up to weakness—hearts. This involves leading the suit that South has bid, but East is correctly leading *through* strength and up to weakness.

South must develop the hearts to make his contract, so he finesses the queen or the ten of hearts, losing to West. Naturally, West wins the trick as cheaply as possible.

Having won the second trick with a heart, West returns to spades, again leading through dummy's strength. The fact that South was unable to win the first trick shows clearly that South was weak in spades. Hence West, too, knows that he is not only leading through strength but also up to weakness.

Declarer must try some sort of finesse in spades, as before, and East wins the trick as cheaply as possible. Once more East shifts to a heart, leading through strength and up to weakness.

South must try a second heart finesse, and West again wins. West leads his last spade, and South is in trouble no matter what he does. He can make only one spade trick, three hearts, and two tricks in each of the minor suits. This comes to only eight tricks, and South should therefore be set one trick.

However, South will probably make his contract against inexperienced defenders if he simply goes up with the ace of spades at this late moment, discarding a diamond from his hand, and enters his hand with the king of diamonds in order to run his three good hearts. It is very hard for the defenders to co-operate with each other in keeping three suits 'sewn up' tightly while making discards on a long suit. Even experts sometimes go wrong in this sort of situation.

South's plan is to discard two low clubs from the dummy to start with. He still holds A-10-2 of clubs in his own hand, and he will be able to establish the ten by cashing the ace and king if the opponents discard too many *clubs*. He has also kept A-10-6 of diamonds in the dummy, and he will be able to establish dummy's ten of diamonds by cashing the ace and king if the opponents discard too many *diamonds*.

Dummy also still has a spade. East must keep his last spade as long as dummy keeps the low spade!

The defenders *can* save the right cards. East must throw one diamond and one club to begin with. For his third discard, East must throw whatever dummy discards. And West must discard a diamond on the fifth heart.

Note that East keeps queen and two small diamonds, so West doesn't have to keep that suit protected. East discards a club, so West must save *his* clubs. The general principle is that each partner saves one suit. If they both try to save the same suit, they will have to give up some other suit, and that will give the declarer the trick he is looking for.

This kind of play is known as a 'squeeze'. Don't think too much about it at this stage of your game, because it is the most difficult of all plays to execute properly, and also the most difficult to defend against. But it won't do you any harm to notice the benefits that you may get as declarer when you lead out a long suit. And it's also a good idea to get the general idea of the defence—to keep the suit that your partner does *not* keep.

Now let's go back to the opening lead. West was reluctant to open a club or a diamond because he was afraid of losing a trick in whichever suit he led. He was quite right.

When the high cards of a suit are scattered round the table, it often costs a trick to whichever side first leads the suit. If you wait for the opponents to begin the suit, *they* lose the trick.

Suppose West leads a low diamond, for example. Dummy plays low, and East must play the queen to prevent South from winning with the nine of diamonds. Now South can lead a diamond from his hand and finesse dummy's ten. He is sure to make three diamond tricks because West's lead allowed him to capture the queen.

Now suppose that East leads a low diamond after he wins the first trick with a spade. South plays low, and West must put up the knave to prevent dummy from winning with the ten. Now dummy can lead a low diamond, and South can finesse the nine. South wins three diamond tricks because East's lead allowed him to capture the knave.

The situation is much the same in clubs. A club lead by either defender would allow South to win three high clubs (and then dummy's fourth club would be good as well).

In this case, if the defenders avoid leading the minor suits, South will eventually have to tackle them. If South leads either suit, he can take the ace and king, but then he will have to lose a trick to the queen or knave.

West thought spades might turn out well because North had not rebid the suit and South had failed to raise it. This sounded as though dummy didn't have *too* much in spades, and West could tell in advance that he would probably be leading through strength and up to weakness. This is often true when you lead through *dummy's* bid suit. Beware, however, of leading a suit that dummy has bid more than once; such a suit will usually be long and strong. Beware, also, of leading *declarer's* bid suit; you will then be leading up to strength instead of up to weakness.

The Duck by a Defender

56.

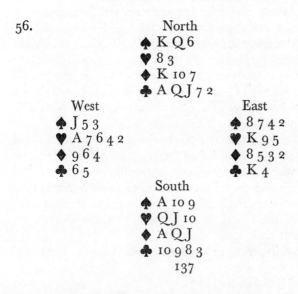

North
♠ K Q 6
♥ 8 3
♦ K 10 7
♣ A Q J 7 2

West
♠ J 5 3
♥ A 7 6 4 2
♦ 9 6 4
♣ 6 5

East
♠ 8 7 4 2
♥ K 9 5
♦ 8 5 3 2
♣ K 4

South
♠ A 10 9
♥ Q J 10
♦ A Q J
♣ 10 9 8 3

The bidding:

North	East	South	West
1 ♣	Pass	2 NT	Pass
3 NT	Pass	Pass	Pass

West opens the four of hearts, fourth-highest card of his long suit. Dummy plays a low heart, and East wins the first trick with the king. East returns the nine of hearts (his highest card in partner's led suit), and South plays the queen of hearts. The fate of the defence now depends on whether West takes the trick with his ace of hearts or allows South to win the trick.

If West wins the trick, his hand is then dead! A third round of hearts must be led to knock out declarer's stopper and now West's hand is quite worthless. West has no outside entry, and East has no hearts to lead back to him.

See how it works out. West takes the second trick with the ace of hearts and returns a heart. South wins with the knave of hearts and tries the club finesse. East takes the king of clubs, but cannot do any damage. He has no hearts left, and the other suits are controlled by declarer. South makes ten tricks, losing only two hearts and one club.

How does it work out if West refuses to win the second trick with his ace of hearts? South must try the club finesse in order to have any chance for his contract. East wins with the king of clubs *and still has a heart to lead.*

Now West can take the trick with the ace of hearts and can cash the two established hearts. The defenders set the contract with four hearts and one club.

Perhaps you remember the ducking play that was used by the declarer in Hand No. 20. West has made use of exactly the same play in this case. The duck is sauce for the goose as well as for the gander.

Incidentally, note that South tried to panic West into

taking the ace of hearts too soon. South played the *queen* of hearts at the second trick instead of the knave of hearts. A foolish West might think that South didn't have the knave of hearts, and that the suit was already established.

A wise West would look at the card that his partner returned at the second trick—the *nine* of hearts. This is known to be East's *highest* heart. Hence East cannot have the knave of hearts. (If East held K-J-9-5 of hearts, he would win the first trick with the king and return the *five* of hearts, his original fourth-highest card. If he held K-J-9, he would win the first trick with the king and return the jack at the second trick. The rule is to return the highest possible card when you hold only two or three.)

South's attempt at deception—his play of the *queen* of hearts at the second trick—is called a 'false card'. In most cases you can protect yourself against a false card if you examine your partner's play very carefully and then trust your partner (if he is a reliable player) rather than the opponent.

THE HOLD-UP BY A DEFENDER

57.

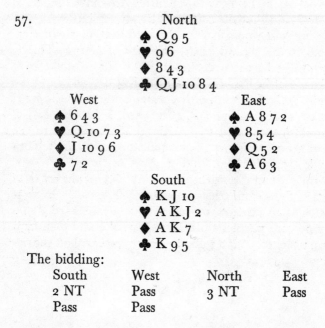

North
- ♠ Q 9 5
- ♥ 9 6
- ♦ 8 4 3
- ♣ Q J 10 8 4

West
- ♠ 6 4 3
- ♥ Q 10 7 3
- ♦ J 10 9 6
- ♣ 7 2

East
- ♠ A 8 7 2
- ♥ 8 5 4
- ♦ Q 5 2
- ♣ A 6 3

South
- ♠ K J 10
- ♥ A K J 2
- ♦ A K 7
- ♣ K 9 5

The bidding:

South	West	North	East
2 NT	Pass	3 NT	Pass
Pass	Pass		

West opens the knave of diamonds, the top of a sequence. South wins the first trick with the king of diamonds and leads the king of clubs. He wants to force out the ace of clubs and then run the rest of dummy's clubs. If East takes the ace of clubs, South will easily win four club tricks. The defenders will win, at most, one club, one spade, and two diamonds.

East must refuse the first club trick! South now leads the nine of clubs and overtakes with dummy's queen, hoping to coax East to take the ace of clubs at the second trick. But East refuses the second club trick as well!

Declarer leads a third club from the dummy, and East must take the ace this time. East returns the queen of diamonds (his highest card in West's suit), and South holds up. East continues with his last diamond, and South wins with the ace.

Do you see what is happening? East has held up the ace of clubs, and South has held up the ace of diamonds. The hand is a battle of hold-ups.

Now South has to find a way to get to dummy for the rest of the club tricks. The queen of spades is the only possible entry, so South leads the king of spades from his hand.

East must refuse to take the trick. If he takes the ace of spades, South can later lead the ten of spades to Dummy's queen, after which the two good clubs can be cashed.

South now leads the knave of spades and plays the queen of spades from the dummy. (This play would work if *West* had the ace of spades.) East must take the ace now, because otherwise declarer would cash the club tricks at once. East isn't holding up just for the sake of holding-up; he wants to keep declarer out of the dummy, and he was saving the ace of spades to play whenever dummy played the queen.

East returns a heart, and South's only remaining chance is to try the finesse. The knave of hearts loses to West's queen, and West cashes his last diamond to set the contract. East's two hold-ups had the effect of killing the dummy, and South couldn't make nine tricks with his own hand all by itself.

The duck in Hand No. 56 and this hold-up resemble each other, but there is an important difference. You duck to save your own entry, but you hold up in order to destroy an opponent's entry.

Unblocking by a Defender

Very nearly the first thing you learn as a declarer is to get the short hand's high cards out of the way so that the long hand can then win the rest of the tricks in a suit without being blocked. The same principle applies in defensive play!

58.

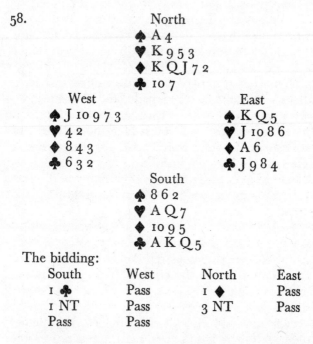

The bidding:

South	West	North	East
1 ♣	Pass	1 ♦	Pass
1 NT	Pass	3 NT	Pass
Pass	Pass		

West opens the knave of spades, and South plays the four of spades from the dummy. If East plays his low spade, West's knave of spades will win the first trick. It may seem wasteful for East to play the queen of spades when his partner's knave is good enough to win the trick, but East must be ready to sacrifice his own high cards for a worthwhile cause. In this case if East plays his low spade, South will make the contract.

Let's see how it works out if East plays his low spade at the first trick.

West wins the first trick with the knave of spades and leads another spade (no other lead will do any good). Dummy wins with the ace.

South leads a small diamond from the dummy in order to knock out the ace of diamonds. East takes his ace of diamonds and can now cash his remaining spade trick, but there is no way he can put West into the lead to cash the established spade tricks. The defenders thus take two spades and one diamond—and South takes all the rest.

Now let's see what happens when East correctly plays the queen of spades at the first trick. He wins that trick, of course, and must then return the *king* of spades to knock out dummy's ace!

It is perfectly true that East's *small* spade would do just as good a job of knocking out dummy's ace. East leads the king because he wants to get his high card out of the way. (This sort of play is called *unblocking*.)

Declarer wins the second spade trick with dummy's ace and leads a diamond to knock out the ace. East takes the ace of diamonds and can now lead the carefully preserved *five* of spades for West to overtake.

Thanks to East's unblocking manœuvre, West is able to win the trick and cash the rest of his spade suit. The defenders thus win four spades and a diamond, setting the contract. East's careful unblock makes a difference of *two* defensive tricks.

FIVE

Defending Against Trump Contracts

As we have seen, the basic principle of the defence against a no-trump contract is the establishment and cashing of a long suit. This principle will seldom help you when you are defending against trump contracts. Declarer's trump suit will usually act as a barrier against your long suit.

Since you cannot expect to win tricks with your low cards against a trump contract, you must be exceptionally careful with your *high* cards. For example, you avoid leading away from a suit that is headed by the ace; at no-trumps, however, that would be a very fine opening lead.

It is still important to lead through strength and up to weakness. You follow many of the principles that help you in the defence against no-trump contracts. But the game is more a matter of getting a trick here and a trick there than of hammering away at a long suit with the idea of running it eventually for the bulk of the defensive tricks.

By way of compensation for losing *length* values, you get something extra in the shape of *shortness* values. Sometimes your best defence is to play for the ruff of one of declarer's good cards with an otherwise worthless trump. This may involve opening a singleton or a doubleton in the hope of getting the ruff before declarer can draw all of your trumps.

Sometimes you don't deliberately go out for the ruff, but have it thrust on you as declarer tries to develop his tricks.

Sometimes you have reason to believe that declarer will try to ruff his losing cards in the dummy, or that he will play the hand as a cross-ruff. In such a case you often find that the best defence is to lead a trump and to keep hammering away at the trumps as often as you get the chance to do so.

Then there's the sort of hand that follows the opposite principle. You lead a long suit of your own with the intention of making declarer ruff in his own hand (*not* in the dummy). If you can make him ruff often enough, you may wind up with more trumps than he has, and you may thus cause him to lose control of the hand.

In short, the defence against a trump contract is more complex than the defence against a no-trump contract. Declarer usually has more ways of playing the hand, and you usually have more ways of defending.

The opening lead is selected in much the same way as in the defence against no-trumps. If possible, you lead your partner's bid suit. If your partner hasn't bid, you usually lead an unbid suit. You avoid leading a suit headed by the ace, and you're not very fond of leading away from a king. You don't want to lose a trick by the lead, because that trick may never come back to you.

You still lead the highest card of a sequence—the king from a suit headed by K-Q-J or by K-Q-10; the queen from a suit headed by Q-J-10 or by Q-J-9; and the knave from a suit headed by J-10-9 or by J-10-8. You may also lead the king from a suit headed by A-K. (Hence the lead of the king shows that the leader also has either the ace or the queen.)

You avoid leading *any* card from a suit headed by A-Q-J or by A-J-10 or by K-J-10. Such leads are too likely to cost you a trick. You may lead the king from a suit headed by K-Q-x, but you aren't especially fond of such a lead.

In leading your partner's suit, follow the same principles as you would at no-trumps. A singleton (a desirable opening lead) gives you no choice. With a doubleton, lead the higher card. With three or four headed by touching honours, lead the top honour; otherwise lead low. However, do *not* lead a low card when you have the ace of your partner's suit. If you decide to lead the suit, lay down the ace to begin with.

Leading Your Partner's Suit

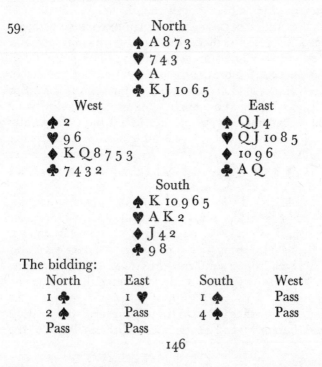

59.

North
♠ A 8 7 3
♥ 7 4 3
♦ A
♣ K J 10 6 5

West
♠ 2
♥ 9 6
♦ K Q 8 7 5 3
♣ 7 4 3 2

East
♠ Q J 4
♥ Q J 10 8 5
♦ 10 9 6
♣ A Q

South
♠ K 10 9 6 5
♥ A K 2
♦ J 4 2
♣ 9 8

The bidding:

North	East	South	West
1 ♣	1 ♥	1 ♠	Pass
2 ♠	Pass	4 ♠	Pass
Pass	Pass		

West should have no problem about his opening lead. East has bid hearts, and West should therefore lead a heart. With a doubleton in his partner's suit, West properly leads the higher card—the nine of hearts.

This opening lead gets the defenders off to a good start in a race against the declarer. The defenders are trying to set up and cash a heart trick. Meanwhile, the declarer is trying to set up dummy's clubs in order to discard his losing heart.

South wins the first trick with the king of hearts and draws two rounds of trumps with the ace and king. He is disappointed with the 3-1 trump break. (If the trumps had been 2-2, South would have lost no trump trick.)

South next leads the nine of clubs from his hand and lets it ride for a finesse. He is pretty sure that East has the ace of clubs, since East has bid, but he hopes that West has the *queen*.

East wins the club trick with his queen, and returns the queen of hearts. He is still trying to establish a heart trick before South can discard a heart on dummy's clubs.

South must win the heart return with his ace and must now go down as gracefully as possible. He leads another club, but East takes the ace of clubs and cashes the knave of hearts. He also gets his trump trick sooner or later, taking a trump, a heart, and two clubs to defeat the contract.

South would have made his contract if the defenders had relaxed at any time. They had to keep plugging away at hearts to get their heart trick. They weren't trying to establish the whole suit, as they would be at no-trumps; they were just trying to develop one trick in the suit.

Suppose, for example, that West foolishly opens a diamond instead of the nine of hearts. Dummy wins with the ace of diamonds, and South gets to his hand with the king of spades to try a club finesse. East takes the queen of clubs and returns the queen of hearts, but it is too late.

South takes the king of hearts, cashes the ace of spades, and then gives up a club trick. Declarer still has the ace of hearts, and nothing can stop him from getting back to dummy with a diamond ruff to discard his losing heart on a high club.

Similarly, South makes the contract even against the heart opening lead if East relaxes. South wins the first heart with the king and takes two trumps and a club finesse. East wins with the queen of clubs and foolishly returns a diamond. Dummy wins with the ace of diamonds and returns a club. Now nothing can stop declarer from getting back to dummy with a diamond ruff to discard his losing heart on a high club.

LEADING AN UNBID SUIT

60.

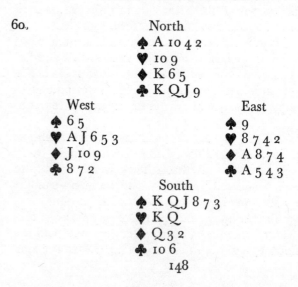

North
♠ A 10 4 2
♥ 10 9
♦ K 6 5
♣ K Q J 9

West
♠ 6 5
♥ A J 6 5 3
♦ J 10 9
♣ 8 7 2

East
♠ 9
♥ 8 7 4 2
♦ A 8 7 4
♣ A 5 4 3

South
♠ K Q J 8 7 3
♥ K Q
♦ Q 3 2
♣ 10 6

DEFENDING AGAINST TRUMP CONTRACTS

The bidding:

North	East	South	West
1 ♣	Pass	1 ♠	Pass
2 ♠	Pass	4 ♠	Pass
Pass	Pass		

West has no partnership bid to help him. He decides to steer away from the black suits, since those have been bid by the enemy. He must therefore choose between the red suits for his opening lead.

West shies away from hearts because it may cost him a trick to lead a suit headed by the ace. The diamonds provide a fairly safe lead and combine a slight element of attack with safety. Hence West opens the knave of diamonds.

Declarer plays a low diamond from the dummy at the first trick, and East must *not* play the ace. He must save the ace to capture dummy's king. Hence East signals encouragement by playing the *eight* of diamonds.

We must now stop and look at this defensive signal. When you are not trying to win a trick, you may play a higher card than necessary to signal encouragement to your partner. If you play the lowest possible card, you indicate one of three things:

(*a*) definite discouragement; or

(*b*) no particular opinion, and therefore no willingness to encourage your partner to lead the suit again; or

(*c*) inability to spare a higher card for fear of losing a trick because of the signal.

Sometimes you have to play a high card because you have nothing lower; and sometimes you have to play a low card because you can't afford to spare anything bigger. Most of the time, however, your signal will be perfectly clear to your partner—*if he is watching for your signals*. Even the clearest signal means nothing to an unobservant partner.

DEFENDING AGAINST TRUMP CONTRACTS

South wins the first trick with the queen of diamonds, draws two rounds of trumps, and leads a club to knock out the ace. East wins the ace of clubs and thus gets the first defensive trick. He knows that three more defensive tricks are needed to defeat the contract.

Having counted in this way, East knows that the defence is doomed unless his partner can win at least one heart trick. There is certainly no hurry about taking the diamond ace.

Hence East returns the deuce of hearts. (This is his fourth highest card. Some good players would lead the *eight* of hearts, indicating by the 'top of nothing' lead that the hand has no heart strength.) West takes the ace of hearts and remembers that East played the encouraging eight of diamonds on the first trick. So West shifts back to the ten of diamonds, and the defenders take two diamond tricks to defeat the contract.

As you can see, the defenders took a double finesse in diamonds to defeat this contract. Finesses work just as well for the defenders as for the declarer.

LEADING THROUGH DUMMY'S BID SUIT

61.

North
♠ 5 4 2
♥ A Q J 9
♦ K Q J 5
♣ A 4

West
♠ K J 9 3
♥ 6 5
♦ A 10 6 2
♣ Q 10 7

East
♠ 7
♥ K 10 8 7
♦ 9 8 7 4 3
♣ 6 5 2

South
♠ A Q 10 8 6
♥ 4 3 2
♦ ——
♣ K J 9 8 3

The bidding:

North	East	South	West
1 ♥	Pass	1 ♠	Pass
2 ♦	Pass	3 ♣	Pass
3 NT	Pass	4 ♣	Pass
4 ♠	Pass	Pass	Pass

West cannot lead an unbid suit, because all the suits have been bid. Dummy has bid both of the red suits, and declarer has bid both of the black suits. West should not lead up to strength, so he must not lead either of the suits that declarer has bid. He must choose one of the red suits.

The choice is fairly easy. West knows that dummy has diamond strength behind him. A diamond lead will therefore serve only to help set up dummy's suit. West doesn't know much about the heart situation, but there is a fair chance that East as well as North has some heart strength. If this is so, a heart lead through dummy will put East in favourable playing position.

This is a roundabout way of saying that you try to lead through (dummy's) strength and *towards* (partner's) strength. You don't want to lead towards *nothing*.

Hence West opens the six of hearts. The rule is always the same for leading a doubleton—lead the higher card.

South must try to finesse of the queen of hearts, and East wins with the king. The heart lead therefore turns out exactly as West has hoped.

The rest of the hand is mostly an exercise in playing the trump suit. West must make sure of getting his three trump tricks to defeat the contract.

At the second trick, East has an easy trump return. (A very fine player would actually return a diamond, even though dummy has such strength in diamonds, reasoning as follows: 'It is clear from the bidding that South has at least ten black cards; and from the opening lead, that South has two or three hearts. Obviously South is very short in diamonds—quite possibly void. If South has a singleton small diamond, it may be vital for us to take the ace before South manages to discard that diamond loser on one of dummy's high hearts.')

If East returns a trump South finesses the queen, losing to West's king. West leads his remaining heart, and dummy wins. Declarer takes the ace and king of clubs, and ruffs a club in dummy, establishing the rest of his suit. He then leads dummy's last trump, hoping to win a finesse or at least to clear the suit without losing more than two trump tricks altogether.

As it happens, East shows out on the second round of trumps, and South can do nothing to avoid the loss of two more trump tricks.

Incidentally, South would have made his contract if West had made the mistake of leading the ace of diamonds. South would ruff and would be able to discard his losing hearts on dummy's good diamonds. South would lose three trump tricks, but nothing else.

LEADING A SINGLETON FOR A RUFFING TRICK

62.

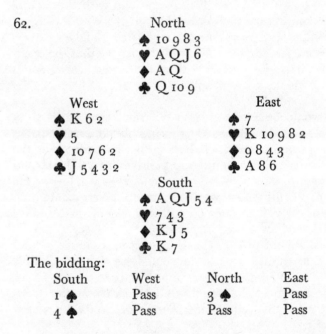

North
♠ 10 9 8 3
♥ A Q J 6
♦ A Q
♣ Q 10 9

West
♠ K 6 2
♥ 5
♦ 10 7 6 2
♣ J 5 4 3 2

East
♠ 7
♥ K 10 9 8 2
♦ 9 8 4 3
♣ A 8 6

South
♠ A Q J 5 4
♥ 7 4 3
♦ K J 5
♣ K 7

The bidding:

South	West	North	East
1 ♠	Pass	3 ♠	Pass
4 ♠	Pass	Pass	Pass

West leads the singleton five of hearts, hoping to develop a ruffing trick. A singleton is not always a desirable opening lead because it often hits declarer's best side suit and traps some honour (such as the queen or knave) held by the leader's partner. A singleton has the further disadvant-

153

age of handing over the control to declarer instead of developing defensive tricks. But a singleton is likely to be a good lead when the strong bidding of the enemy or the weakness of your own hand make desperation measures seem attractive. In this case, certainly, West has so weak a hand that he is justified in trying almost anything.

South suspects that the opening lead is a singleton and therefore goes right up with dummy's ace of hearts. (If South took the finesse, East would win with the king of hearts and return the suit at once to give West a ruff.)

South craftily drops the seven of hearts (a false card) on the first trick, hoping that East will believe that the opening leader holds one or both of the lower hearts. South then leads the three of spades to the ace and returns the four of spades!

It would be hard to blame West for being deceived by this play. A thoughtless West would play the six of spades at the second trump trick, hoping that East could win the trick with the knave or queen. But if West played his second low trump, dummy would win, and West would lose the chance to ruff with a worthless trump. (West would gain nothing by ruffing later on with the *king* of spades, since that is good for a trick anyway.)

West should put up the king of spades on the second round of trumps because he should see through South's little plot. If South held only four trumps to the ace-knave or the ace-queen, he would surely take a trump finesse instead of playing out his ace. The failure to finesse is very revealing.

If West is clever enough to put up the king of spades on the second round of trumps, he must now find a way to get to the East hand for the heart ruff. How does West know whether to lead a club or a diamond to get to the East hand?

This is easier than it looks. For one thing, the ace of diamonds is in plain sight in the dummy. West knows that declarer would be happy to win a trick at this moment with the diamond ace, in order to draw the last trump. Moreover, an alert East will have helped his partner by discarding the eight of clubs on the second round of trumps. This high card shows club strength—in this case, a fast club entry.

West obediently leads a club, and East takes the ace. East next cashes the king of hearts, and West discards a small club. East finally leads a third heart, and West ruffs. Thus the contract is defeated.

The contract would have been made if West had led anything but the singleton heart. South could well afford to lose a trump, a club and (eventually) a heart. It was the heart ruff that beat him.

LEADING A DOUBLETON TO GET A RUFF

63.

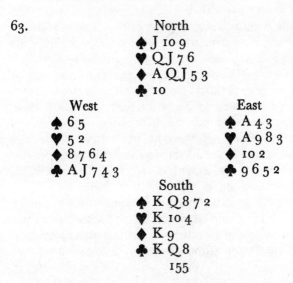

```
                 North
               ♠ J 10 9
               ♥ Q J 7 6
               ♦ A Q J 5 3
               ♣ 10
   West                        East
  ♠ 6 5                       ♠ A 4 3
  ♥ 5 2                       ♥ A 9 8 3
  ♦ 8 7 6 4                   ♦ 10 2
  ♣ A J 7 4 3                 ♣ 9 6 5 2
                 South
               ♠ K Q 8 7 2
               ♥ K 10 4
               ♦ K 9
               ♣ K Q 8
```

The bidding:

South	West	North	East
1 ♠	Pass	2 ♦	Pass
2 NT	Pass	3 ♠	Pass
4 ♠	Pass	Pass	Pass

West has no reason to lead diamonds or spades, so must lead one of the unbid suits. The clubs are awkward (as always in the case of a suit headed by the ace), so West therefore decides to lead a heart. The correct lead when you hold a doubleton is the higher card, so West leads the five of hearts.

Declarer plays a low heart from the dummy, and East takes the ace and hopefully returns the suit. He doesn't really believe that West has led a singleton, but there is always the chance.

South wins the second heart trick in the dummy and leads the knave of spades. As East, what would you do? You should hop up with the ace of spades at once! The general rule is *second hand low*, but in this case you cannot afford to wait. You have to give your partner a ruff while he still has a trump left.

After winning the first trump trick with the ace of spades, East leads a third round of hearts. West is able to ruff this, thus collecting the third defensive trick. West then promptly cashes the ace of clubs to make sure of setting the contract. (If West failed to take the setting trick at once, South would regain the lead, draw the last trump and run the diamonds to discard all three of his clubs. This would make West look very foolish!)

You probably noticed that South would have made his contract if East had played low on the first round of trumps. The knave of spades would hold the first trump trick (if East played low), and dummy would continue with another trump. This would remove West's last trump and thus kill his chance to make a ruffing trick.

There's another point of interest in this hand. East could afford to take the first heart trick because he knew that he could regain the lead quickly with the ace of spades. It therefore cost him nothing to play West for a singleton heart.

The situation would be different if you exchanged the ace of trumps for the five of trumps. In other words, let's give West the ace and six of spades, and give East three small trumps. Now when West leads the five of hearts, East must not take his ace at once. (If he does, he can return a heart, but West is not yet ready to ruff. East never regains the lead, declarer pulls trumps, and West's ruffing trick is lost.) East must *duck* the first heart trick, playing the nine to show that he has strength in the suit. Declarer immediately goes after the trumps, and it is now West who takes the ace. West then leads his remaining deuce of hearts—and *this* time East takes the ace and immediately leads back a third round of hearts for West to ruff.

LEADING A TRUMP

64.

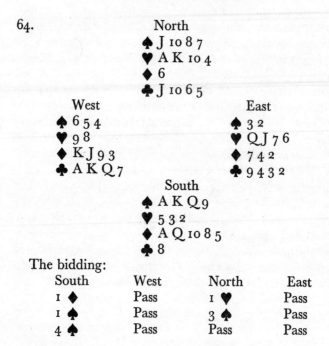

North
♠ J 10 8 7
♥ A K 10 4
♦ 6
♣ J 10 6 5

West
♠ 6 5 4
♥ 9 8
♦ K J 9 3
♣ A K Q 7

East
♠ 3 2
♥ Q J 7 6
♦ 7 4 2
♣ 9 4 3 2

South
♠ A K Q 9
♥ 5 3 2
♦ A Q 10 8 5
♣ 8

The bidding:

South	West	North	East
1 ♦	Pass	1 ♥	Pass
1 ♠	Pass	3 ♠	Pass
4 ♠	Pass	Pass	Pass

If the bidding were different West would be delighted to open the king of clubs. Such a lead from a suit headed by ace-king-queen provides an ideal attack and is also safe.

In this case, however, the lead of the king of clubs would not be safe. North's bidding indicates good support for spades. It also hints at shortness in diamonds, South's first bid suit, and West's own diamond holding confirms this diagnosis. (South and West probably have nine of the thirteen diamonds between them.) West reasons that South will probably try to ruff his losing diamonds in the dummy. In order to reduce dummy's ruffing power, West therefore leads a trump.

West's opening lead, the six of spades, strikes a body blow at South's contract. South cannot quite manage to get ten tricks.

Declarer wins the first trick, cashes the ace of diamonds, and ruffs a diamond in the dummy. Now he has to get to his own hand to continue the ruffing process.

How does South get back to his hand without further shortening his trumps? Well, first he leads the knave of clubs from the dummy, intending to cross-ruff. West wins with the queen of clubs and then leads a second trump, continuing with his plan.

South wins and ruffs another diamond in the dummy. But that uses up dummy's last trump, and West still holds the king of diamonds!

What can South do next? He can ruff a club, if he likes, and draw the last trump. But now the long diamonds will never come in. South will make four trumps in his own hand, two ruffs in the dummy, the ace of diamonds, and two top hearts. The total is only nine tricks.

The situation is quite different if West makes the mistake of opening the king of clubs. Even if West immediately shifts to a trump, he is too late!

Let's see how it works out. South wins the second trick with a high trump, cashes the ace of diamonds and ruffs a diamond in the dummy. Now he gets back to his hand easily by ruffing a club. There is no need to give a defender the chance to lead a second trump!

So South cashes the top hearts and ruffs diamonds in the dummy and ruffs clubs in his own hand. He wins four trumps of his own, three ruffs in the dummy, two top hearts, and the ace of diamonds. The total is ten tricks, exactly what South needs for his game contract. The moral

DEFENDING AGAINST TRUMP CONTRACTS

is quite plain: If the bidding calls for a trump lead, don't delay. Lead a trump at once.

The High-Low

65.

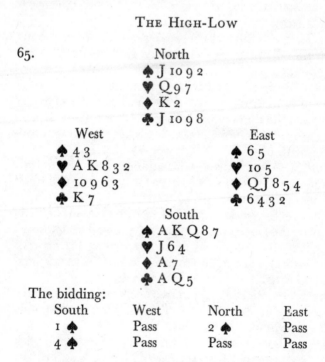

West North East
```
              North
              ♠ J 10 9 2
              ♥ Q 9 7
              ♦ K 2
              ♣ J 10 9 8
  West                      East
  ♠ 4 3                     ♠ 6 5
  ♥ A K 8 3 2               ♥ 10 5
  ♦ 10 9 6 3                ♦ Q J 8 5 4
  ♣ K 7                     ♣ 6 4 3 2
              South
              ♠ A K Q 8 7
              ♥ J 6 4
              ♦ A 7
              ♣ A Q 5
```

The bidding:

South	West	North	East
1 ♠	Pass	2 ♠	Pass
4 ♠	Pass	Pass	Pass

West opens the king of hearts. This is a fairly good attacking lead, and there is nothing in the bidding to steer West away from this perfectly sound opening lead.

Dummy plays the seven of hearts, East plays the *ten* of hearts, and South drops the *knave* of hearts.

West wonders what is going on. Did South hold a singleton knave of hearts? If so, it would be very dangerous to lead a second round of the suit.

But if South held a singleton knave of hearts, that would give the rest of the missing hearts to East. And East would then have started with 10-6-5-4 of the suit. Why would East play the ten of hearts if he held four hearts headed by the ten?

The answer is very simple. East wouldn't dream of playing the ten of hearts in that case. Hence East cannot hold all of the missing hearts. South must obviously be trying out some monkey business in order to confuse the defenders.

Before we go on with West's next play, let's see why East really does play the ten of hearts. East wasn't trying to win the trick, and he played a higher heart than necessary. This means: 'Partner, lead the suit again'.

Sometimes a defender will signal in this way because he has Q-x-x and hopes to take the third trick with his queen. Sometimes he signals encouragement because he has a doubleton and hopes to ruff the third round with an otherwise worthless trump.

Mind you, East's signal doesn't indicate a specific holding. It means that East wants his partner to continue the suit. In some cases, the leader's partner may urgently want a shift to a different suit even if he holds the queen or a doubleton in the suit that has been opened. If he wants a shift, he does not begin a high-low.

In this case it is easy for West to read the meaning of the ten of hearts. East is obviously beginning a high-low with a doubleton in hearts. West counts the hearts carefully, giving his partner credit for only two of them. This means that South originally held three hearts. Hence East will be able to ruff the third round of hearts *safely*. West would not necessarily lead a third heart if he knew the declarer would also be out of the suit and would be able to over-ruff East.

In this case West can see that all is plain sailing. He wins the first trick with the king of hearts, continues with the ace of hearts to win the second trick, and then leads a third heart. East ruffs the third heart, thus winning the third defensive trick. South must eventually give a club trick to West, and the contract is thus defeated.

If the defenders had failed to get this ruffing trick, South would have made his contract. Declarer would have drawn trumps and set up the clubs, losing only two hearts and a club.

THE FORCING GAME

It is sometimes possible to *outlast* declarer with your trumps. This happens most often when you have four or more trumps to begin with, and when you can make declarer ruff once or twice *in his own hand*.

It is important to notice those last four words. It is usually to declarer's advantage to ruff in the dummy. Making declarer ruff in his own hand, however, does nothing for him that he couldn't do for himself. It is therefore a good idea to force declarer to ruff in his own hand if you have enough trump length to make trouble for him.

66.

North
♠ 6 4
♥ A 10 5
♦ K Q J 10 4
♣ K J 9

West
♠ K 5 3 2
♥ K Q J 9 7 4
♦ A 8
♣ 6

East
♠ 8 7
♥ 3 2
♦ 7 6 3 2
♣ 7 5 4 3 2

South
♠ A Q J 10 9
♥ 8 6
♦ 9 5
♣ A Q 10 8

The bidding:

North	East	South	West
1 ♦	Pass	1 ♠	2 ♥
Pass	Pass	3 ♠	Pass
3 NT	Pass	4 ♠	Pass
Pass	Pass		

West opens the king of hearts, and dummy wins with the ace. Declarer takes the trump finesse, losing the queen to West's king.

West leads the queen of hearts, winning the second defensive trick, and then leads the knave of hearts. South has to ruff because he must eventually lose a trick to the ace of diamonds, and he dare not lose any other tricks.

South now leads a diamond towards dummy without leading a second trump. This is a good idea, as we shall see, but it doesn't work.

West steps right up with the ace of diamonds, taking his

third defensive trick. He needs one more trick to set the contract. He leads a fourth heart!

Dummy ruffs with the six, but East is able to over-ruff with his remaining eight of trumps. South was hoping that East would not be able to over-ruff.

South must win the trick by ruffing still higher. Otherwise, if he fails to ruff this trick, he is set at once.

This leaves South with only two trumps in his hand—and West still has *three* trumps. South started with one trump more than West, but he has been 'forced' (made to ruff) twice, and now he has one trump *less* than West!

South leads the ace of trumps, hoping that both opponents will follow suit, in which case he can draw the last trump and run the rest of the tricks. But West has all three of the missing trumps, and the rest of the hand is very sad for poor South.

No matter how South plays he can now make only his last trump, one diamond, and one club. West will make a trump and two heart tricks, setting the contract *three* tricks! It does South no good to keep his last trump and lead clubs (or diamonds). West will ruff as soon as possible and lead another heart to punch out South's last trump. West can thus stay one trump ahead of South, keeping control of the hand.

South could have won *nine* sure tricks by leading the trumps and the clubs and leaving the diamonds alone, but his actual line of play gave him the best chance to *make* the contract. A good player tries for his contract, if there is a possibility of making it, even at the risk of going down an extra trick or so!

THE UPPERCUT

67.

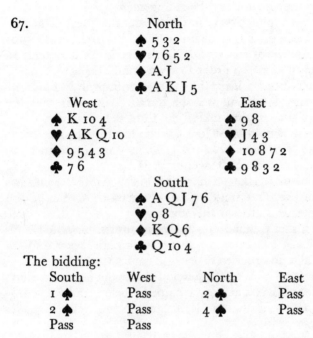

North
♠ 5 3 2
♥ 7 6 5 2
♦ A J
♣ A K J 5

West
♠ K 10 4
♥ A K Q 10
♦ 9 5 4 3
♣ 7 6

East
♠ 9 8
♥ J 4 3
♦ 10 8 7 2
♣ 9 8 3 2

South
♠ A Q J 7 6
♥ 9 8
♦ K Q 6
♣ Q 10 4

The bidding:

South	West	North	East
1 ♠	Pass	2 ♣	Pass
2 ♠	Pass	4 ♠	Pass
Pass	Pass		

West has no trouble selecting his opening lead—the king of hearts. Such leads are usually ideal, and it should be kept in mind that the trump lead recommended in Hand No. 64 is quite exceptional and well marked by the bidding, and certainly a lead away from the king-ten is highly unattractive. In this case there is nothing in the bidding to steer West away from his normal opening lead.

West wins the first trick with his king of hearts and continues the suit. At the second trick he leads the queen of hearts. West is not discouraged by the fact that East played

165

the three of hearts at the first trick. East cannot afford to encourage a heart continuation, but West's holding is so strong that it needs no encouragement.

After winning the second trick with the queen of hearts, West leads the ace of hearts at the third trick. South ruffs with the six of spades and leads the six of diamonds to dummy's knave in order to try a trump finesse.

When dummy leads the deuce of trumps, East plays the eight and South finesses the queen. West wins with the king of spades, thus taking the third defensive trick.

Where should West look for the fourth defensive trick? Should West lead a club in the hope that his partner has the queen? This isn't necessary. If East has the queen of clubs he will make a trick with it (provided that South has as many as three small clubs) regardless of whether or not West leads a club at this moment.

West's only chance lies in leading his last heart. He leads the ten of hearts, and East must be both clever and co-operative in order to defeat the contract.

The ten of hearts is obviously the highest remaining heart. South has already trumped a heart, and will surely trump this one also. But East should play his nine of spades anyway!

East can do himself no good, he reasons, by keeping the nine of spades in his hand. But if he plays it now, he may drive out a spade high enough to do West some good.

And so it turns out. South must over-ruff with the knave of spades. South can then play the ace of spades, catching West's four of spades; but the ten of spades will then be high for the vital fourth defensive trick. Note that East, with his miserable hand, has co-operated to give partner the setting trick!

South makes his contract if East fails to 'uppercut' with the nine of spades. If East tamely discards, South can ruff with the seven of spades, draw trumps with the ace and knave, and claim the contract.

A Choice of Evils

In some hands all of your leads or plays seem equally undesirable. It is considered unsporting to tear the cards up or walk out of the game, so all you can do is choose the lead or play that seems least harmful.

68.

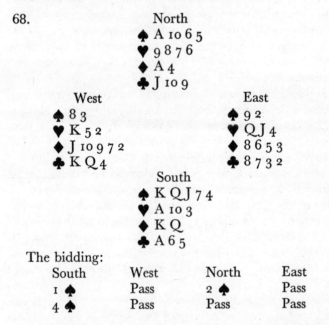

North
♠ A 10 6 5
♥ 9 8 7 6
♦ A 4
♣ J 10 9

West
♠ 8 3
♥ K 5 2
♦ J 10 9 7 2
♣ K Q 4

East
♠ 9 2
♥ Q J 4
♦ 8 6 5 3
♣ 8 7 3 2

South
♠ K Q J 7 4
♥ A 10 3
♦ K Q
♣ A 6 5

The bidding:

South	West	North	East
1 ♠	Pass	2 ♠	Pass
4 ♠	Pass	Pass	Pass

West opens the knave of diamonds, and South wins with the queen. South leads out the king and queen of spades to draw trumps, and then leads the king of diamonds to dummy's ace in order to return the knave of clubs for a finesse.

Now imagine that you are West, seeing only your own hand and the dummy. You win the club trick with your queen, and you must select some sort of return lead. What to do?

You are not eager to lead away from your king of hearts or from your king of clubs. Is it safe to return a diamond?

You know that South has no diamonds in the dummy and that he cannot have any diamonds left in his hand. South would not have wasted his king of diamonds on dummy's ace if he had held a small diamond in his hand.

Can you afford to lead a diamond, knowing that there are no diamonds either in the dummy or in the declarer's hand? No. This is usually the *worst* sort of play that you can make as a defender.

If you lead a diamond, South will ruff in the dummy and discard a *losing* heart from his hand. This play (called a 'sluff and ruff') hands South a trick on the proverbial silver platter. There is no way for South to give himself a sluff and ruff—only a foolish defender can be so kind to him.

Hence you must rule out any possibility of returning a diamond. You must choose between clubs and hearts.

From the way that declarer has played the clubs you suspect that he has the ace of clubs in his hand. If so, it will cost you a trick to lead a club away from your king. (If you lead a low club, dummy's ten will win; and if you lead the king, South will take the ace and dummy's ten will win later.)

For lack of anything better, and not because you are overjoyed about it, you return the deuce of hearts. (The heart king is still guarded.) East plays the knave, and South wins with the ace.

This tells you who has the queen of hearts—just as in Hand No. 51. When South next leads a low heart, you can afford to play low, allowing East to win with the queen.

Now it is up to East to do a little thinking. He must not
return a diamond—just as *you* couldn't. He must not lead
a heart, for that will force you to win with the king of
hearts and make a fatal return of either a diamond or a
club. East therefore returns a club, and now you are sure
to make both of your kings to defeat the contract.

Attacking Dummy's Entries

As we have seen in several hands, if you can't take the
enemy's tricks away from him you may still gain by making him take his tricks before they can do him the most
good. When you are the declarer at a no-trump contract,
for example, you often knock out the dangerous opponent's
entries before he manages to establish his suit. As defender
you can adopt the same principle, usually by making
dummy take its tricks before the long suit is set up.

69.

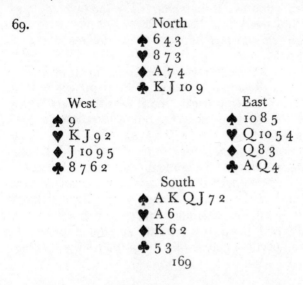

```
                    North
                    ♠ 6 4 3
                    ♥ 8 7 3
                    ♦ A 7 4
                    ♣ K J 10 9
     West                        East
     ♠ 9                         ♠ 10 8 5
     ♥ K J 9 2                   ♥ Q 10 5 4
     ♦ J 10 9 5                  ♦ Q 8 3
     ♣ 8 7 6 2                   ♣ A Q 4
                    South
                    ♠ A K Q J 7 2
                    ♥ A 6
                    ♦ K 6 2
                    ♣ 5 3
```

The bidding:

South	West	North	East
1 ♠	Pass	1 NT	Pass
3 ♠	Pass	3 NT	Pass
4 ♠	Pass	Pass	Pass

West opens the knave of diamonds. South wins in his own hand with the king of diamonds and draws three rounds of trumps. He then leads a club, losing a finesse to East's queen.

What should East return? He is tempted to lead a heart up to dummy's weakness. But it is vital to knock out dummy's only entry, the ace of diamonds, before the clubs have been established. Hence East returns the queen of diamonds.

Dummy wins with the ace of diamonds and returns a club. East takes the ace of clubs, and now the dummy is dead. East can safely lead a heart at this moment, and South can win only his six trump tricks, the two high diamonds, and the ace of hearts. These are nine very fine tricks, but the contract happens to call for ten tricks, so South is down one.

South makes the contract if East leads a heart instead of the queen of diamonds. (This is at the point where East has taken his first club trick.) South wins the heart return with the ace and leads another club to force out the ace. Now the defenders can take one heart trick, but nothing can stop declarer from getting to the dummy with the ace of diamonds to discard the losing diamond on a high club.

Perhaps you wondered how East knew enough to take his two club tricks as soon as they were offered without worrying about the possibility that South might have a third club in his hand. It was partly a matter of sound reasoning and partly a matter of good partnership signalling.

Let's take the reasoning first. East knows that he is going to lead a heart (playing up to weakness) when his ace of clubs is forced out. If South has two losing hearts, he will lose them at that time and the contract will be defeated.

If South has the ace of hearts (which is actually the case) he has one heart, six sure trump tricks (East can count them very easily because he knows that he and dummy started with three each and that West could follow suit only once), and two top diamonds. If South makes one club trick, he will fulfill his contract. East cannot afford to let South make one club trick because of the possibility that he holds the ace of hearts, and doesn't need to let South make one club trick if *West* has the ace of hearts.

The reasoning is logical, but perhaps a bit difficult. Now let's see the signalling.

When South leads the first club, West carefully plays the *eight* of clubs. This is obviously the beginning of our old friend, the high-low.

What does the high-low mean in this case? West cannot hope to ruff, since trumps have been drawn. West cannot be signalling club strength, since East can see all of the high clubs from the ace down to the nine.

West's signal means that he has an *even* number of clubs. (The signal usually shows two or four cards in the suit, but you may get a chance to show a six-card holding once in ten years or so.) If West had an odd number of clubs (especially one, three or five cards in the suit), he would play his lowest club. Then the failure to begin a high-low would tell the story.

Let's repeat it briefly: If West plays his *lowest* card, he shows an odd number of cards in the suit; if West begins a high-low, he shows an even number of cards in the suit.

This signal is reserved for situations in which a player wants to tell his partner when to take an ace. It is common when declarer leads the dummy's long suit, especially when side entries to the dummy are either scarce or non-existent.

In this case, the signal tells East that his partner has an even number of clubs—either two or four. If West has only two clubs, South has four—and the suit cannot possibly be shut out. If West has four clubs, however, South has only two—and then East must take his tricks at once without holding up.

Armed with this knowledge, turn back to Hand No. 57. East is careful to hold up his ace of clubs until the third round of the suit. West played the seven of clubs on the first round of clubs, beginning an obvious high-low. This showed an even number of clubs—two or four. West couldn't have four clubs, because that would give South a singleton, and in that case he wouldn't have bid two no-trumps. It was clear that West had exactly two clubs, which meant that South started with exactly three clubs. Once East had this information it was easy for him to hold up his ace of clubs for precisely the right number of tricks.

(West signalled again when South later led the king of spades in that same hand. West played his *lowest* spade, the three. This showed that West held an odd number of spades. It was easy to work out the exact number: West couldn't have five spades, for then South would have a singleton; West was very unlikely to have only one spade, for then South would have a good five card-major suit. Hence West had three spades, and South also had three.)

All of these signals are very simple to use and simple to read. The only difficulty lies in keeping alert at the bridge table so that you use whichever signal is called for by the situation. If you do that, your partner will likewise keep alert enough to read your signals and co-operate with you in the defence.

DEFENDING AGAINST TRUMP CONTRACTS

No matter how much you may enjoy playing the hand as the declarer, you will eventually find that the greatest satisfactions in bridge come from tight and imaginative defensive play. What's more, it is by far the most important department of the play. You spend about a quarter of your playing time at the bridge table as the dummy, another quarter as the declarer, and *half* as a defender. In other words, you defend twice as often as you play a hand as declarer. Don't neglect a department of the play that occupies so much of your time.

SIX

What to do about Irregularities

Bridge is played by human beings, and human beings make mistakes. Occasionally, therefore, one of the players will lead when it isn't his turn, or will drop a card on the table, or will mistakenly fail to follow suit, or will do something equally silly.

What should you do when any such irregularity takes place?

First, and most important, remember that bridge is a game. Be pleasant about the mishap. Some day you may be the 'offender', and you will be grateful for the good humour and the good sense of the other players.

This doesn't mean that you just smile at an irregularity and pay no attention to it. Many irregularities put the offender's opponents at a disadvantage. In order to overcome this disadvantage, the bridge 'laws' provide penalties for most irregularities.

THE LAWS OF BRIDGE

You may be surprised to learn that it takes a book of fifty pages to set forth the laws of bridge and the penalties for various irregularities. This code of laws is strictly applied in serious matches and in clubs.

Most players get to know the important laws after a

while. Their purpose is to prevent arguments by setting up a standard, reasonable course of action. It isn't necessary to know *all* of the laws. In fact, a player who constantly quotes the laws in a social game becomes deservedly unpopular in a very short time.

You have to use your common sense when an irregularity takes place. If it is obviously a trifle that hasn't put anybody at a disadvantage, pay no attention to it. But if the same person habitually does the wrong thing, or if the irregularity is no trifle, apply the penalty that is prescribed in the laws. The most important penalties are explained in this chapter.

RIGHTS OF THE DUMMY

The dummy should *not* look at his partner's hand or get up to watch declarer play the hand. He shouldn't comment on the play or offer any advice. If the dummy sees that declarer is about to lead from the wrong hand, he may warn him. When an irregularity occurs, dummy may join in the discussion.

PLAYED CARD

A card from the dummy is played as soon as declarer names it or touches it (unless he is clearly pushing it aside to get to another card).

A card from a defender's hand is played when it is put on the table face up or when it is held so that his partner can see it.

A card from the declarer's hand is played when it is put on the table face up.

A played card may not be taken back except to correct an irregularity (such as a revoke).

WHAT TO DO ABOUT IRREGULARITIES

Lead Out of Turn

If the wrong person leads, the correct player may play a card and thus 'regularize' the error. In general, any irregularity may be overlooked by the simple process of continuing with the play as though nothing had happened.

If declarer leads from the wrong hand, either defender may call attention to it. The declarer puts back the false lead and must, if possible, lead the same suit from the correct hand. (He doesn't have to play on that trick the card led from the wrong hand.)

If the wrong defender leads, declarer has his choice of penalties. He may forbid the lead of that suit, in which case the correct leader may lead any of the *other* three suits. Or declarer may let the correct player lead *anything* and may treat the false lead as a 'penalty card'.

If a defender leads or plays two cards at the same time, he may choose either as his correct lead or play. The other card becomes a *penalty card*.

Penalty Cards

If a defender puts or drops a card face up on the table or sees the face of a card that belongs to his partner—except in normal play—any such card becomes a penalty card.

Declarer's cards never becomes penalty cards.

A penalty card is left on the table face up. It must be played at the first legal opportunity. That is, the owner must follow suit with it when the suit is led; or must discard it if he cannot follow the suit that is actually led; or must lead it if he wins a trick.

WHAT TO DO ABOUT IRREGULARITIES

Revokes

A player 'revokes' if he fails to follow suit when able to do so. A revoke becomes 'established' when the offending side leads or plays to the next trick.

To correct a revoke that has *not* been established, the offender takes back the revoke card and follows suit with any correct card. If the offender is one of the defenders, his revoke card is left on the table as a penalty card. The non-offending side may take back any card that was played after the revoke but before its correction.

For example: East, a defender, leads the queen of spades during the course of a hand that South is playing at four hearts. South, the declarer, ruffs with a small heart. West plays a small spade, and dummy plays a small spade also. Now South announces that he has revoked, and he takes back his trump and plays the *king* of spades on the trick. West, if he wishes to do so, may take back his small spade (without leaving it on the table as a penalty card) and play the *ace* of spades on South's king.

Established Revokes: When either player of the 'revoking' side leads or plays to the trick after the revoke, it is too late for a correction. The revoke trick must be left undisturbed, and play continues normally.

At the end of the hand, the offending side transfers two tricks (that were won on or after the revoke) to the other side, and these are scored as though they had been won in natural play. If the offending side won only one trick on or after the revoke, only one trick is transferred. If the offending side won no tricks at all on or after the revoke, there is no penalty. A trick that was won *before* the revoke is never transferred.

For example: South is playing the hand at three hearts.

West opens a spade, and his partner trumps the trick. It later turns out that East has a spade in his hand. The discovery is made one or two tricks later, so the revoke is established. Play continues, and the defenders take five tricks in all. The defenders hand two of their five tricks to South, who then has a total of ten tricks. He scores the hand as though he had won ten tricks in normal play—90 points below the line and 30 points above the line.

Index

INDEX